Thiagi's INTERACTIVE LECTURES

POWER UP Your Training With
Interactive Games and Exercises

 **ASTD Press**

Sivasailam "Thiagi" Thiagarajan

ASTD Press is an internationally renowned source of insightful and practical information on workplace learning and performance topics, including training basics, evaluation and return-on-investment (ROI), instructional systems development (ISD), e-learning, leadership, and career development.

Ordering information: Books published by ASTD Press can be purchased by visiting our Website at store.astd.org or by calling 800.628.2783 or 703.683.8100.

Library of Congress Control Number: 2005926059

ISBN: 1-56286-405-X

Acquisitions and Development Editor: Mark Morrow
Copyeditor: Karen Eddleman
Interior Design and Production: Kathleen Schaner
Cover Design: Ana Ilieva
Cover Illustration: André Craeyvelot of Images.com

Printed by Victor Graphics, Inc., Baltimore, Maryland, www.victorgraphics.com.

Table of Contents

Preface

have three basic beliefs about using games and lectures in training. The first belief is that it's not *either* games or lecture. It's always *both* games and lecture. So, when trainers ask me, "Should I use lectures or training games for becoming a more effective trainer?" I answer, "Yes!"

My second belief is that you want to combine lecture and games, not balance them. You want to blend them. I do not recommend 20 minutes of lectures followed by 20 minutes of games. Instead, I blend appropriate doses of lectures and training games to achieve effective, efficient, and enjoyable learning. With such a seamless blend, participants do not know when I am lecturing and when I am conducting a game. All lectures are positioned as a briefing for the training games that follow or a debriefing of the game that proceeded. Conversely, the training games are positioned as application exercises of the principles and procedures presented in the lectures.

My third belief is that all training materials and methods (including training books) should be designed in collaboration with the eventual users. Many people have contributed to the development of the interactive lecture strategies explored in this book by funding projects, participating in sessions, trying out and improving strategies, providing conceptual inputs, and making sarcastic remarks. I want to thank them all in this book (listed here in alphabetical order by their first names):

Aida Pasigna, Al P. Mizell, Alain Rostain, Andrea Moore, Andrew Kimball, April Davis, Barbara Gough, Barbara L. Blakeslee, Becky Gunn, Ben L. Fox, Bernie DeKoven, Bill Matthews, Bob Wiele, Brandon Carson, Brian Desautels, Brian Remer, Brigid Ferguson, Carl Binder, Carol Haig, Cathy Greenblat, Charles Dupont, Chris Saeger, Chuck Adams, Claire Carey, Clark Aldrich, Craig Perrin, Curtis Jay Bonk, Dale Brethower, Dan Yaman, Daniel C. Roberts, Danny Langdon, Darlene Van Tiem, Darryl Sink, David Crookall, David Gibson, David Gouthro, Dennis Meadows, Diane Dormant, Diane Gayeski, Don Brendley, Don Coombs, Don Tosti, Edward Rowan, Elizabeth Levine, Ellen S. Kay Gehrke, Elsa Glassman, Erica Keeps, Ethan Sanders, Eva Martony, Frances Kemmerer, Gary Muszynski, George Piskurich, Glenn Parker, Goh Abe, Guy Wallace, Harriet Whiting, Heather Robinson, Heidi Fisk, Ivan Cortes, James A. Pershing, Jane Mencer, Jane Sink, Janet Chino, Jeff Lefton, Jennifer Hoffman, Jerry Fountain, Jin Abe, Jodhi Nedungadi, John Walber, Jonathan Heckel, Jonathan Finklestein, Judith Blohm, Julie Groshens, Karen Stoeller, Kat Koppett, Ken Bellemare, Ken Silber, Kim Ruyle, Kim

Zoller, Kit Horton, Kurt Squire, Larry Lipman, Larry Lipsitz, Leah Nelson, Les Lauber, Leslie Brunker, Lindsay Robinson, Lori Gillispie, Lori Ware, Lorraine Ukens, Lou Russell, Lucy Chaddha, Lynn Kearney, Marc Shiman, Margaret Pusch, Margery Auvinen, Mariano Bernardez, Marie Jasinski, Marilyn K. Spatz, Mark Isabella, Mark Wayland, Martin Delahoussaye, Marty Cielens, Mary Broad, Matt Davis, Mel Silberman, Michael Alan, Michael H. Molenda, Miki Lane, Nanette Miner, Patti Shank, Paul Cicco, Paul Cook, Pieter van der Hijden, Rebecca Saeger, Regina Rowland, Richard Pearlstein, Rob Cummins, Rob M. Peck, Robert Horn, Roger Addison, Roger Greenaway, Ruth Clark, Samuel van den Bergh, Sandy Fowler, Saul Carliner, Scott Simmerman, Sharon Bowman, Sharon Ellison, Shaunda Paden, Sonia Ribaux, Steve Sugar, Steve Yelon, Susan Markle, Susan Otto, Tim Scudder, Tom Mucciolo, Tricia Emerson, Tris Brown, Victor Kluck, Will Thalheimer, William Horton, William Wake, and Willy Kriz.

I am sure that I have left out some key contributors. I owe them my apologies—along with my gratitude. I also want to thank thousands of participants who have attended and supported my sessions at a number of conferences including ASTD's annual International Conference and Exposition, International Society for Performance Improvement (ISPI) Training Conference and Expo, the North American Simulation and Gaming Conference (NASAGA), and the International Simulation and Gaming Conference (ISAGA). Through their enthusiastic participation and constructive feedback, they have contributed immensely to the improvement of these interactive lecture designs.

I want to thank Martin for explaining why nobody would want to buy this book. A special thank you is due Marilyn Weishaar (of Weis Revise) for her efficient editing of the initial version of this manuscript. And, of course, I want to thank my wife, Lucy, and the rest of my family: Raja, Julie, Jason, Matt, Kat, and Lia.

Sivasailam "Thiagi" Thiagarajan
July 2005

What's Wrong and What's Right About Lectures?

Lectures are probably the most ridiculed training technique; however, I am not against this instructional method. Looking back on my own training and education, many of my significant learning episodes involved lectures. As a trainer, I have lectured for six solid hours at a time—and still received high ratings on the evaluation sheet. Yet, as trainers, we must admit that lectures have both a positive and negative side.

On the positive side, learners are very comfortable with the method because, no doubt, they have sat through countless lecture classes from grammar school through graduate school. On the negative side, lectures can be just plain boring for the learners. This book will show you a middle road that combines the best features of lecturing with the power of interactive games and exercises. With these tools, you can deliver training that has on-the-job impact for your business and is fun for everyone participating in your class!

Advantages and Disadvantages of the Lecture Method

The reasons the lecture method is popular are obvious. Right or wrong, people believe that lectures have these advantages:

- Lectures are the cultural norm of adult education.
- Lectures inflate the trainer's ego.
- Lectures do not require extensive preparation.
- Lectures permit efficient coverage of content in a limited time.
- Lectures can reach a large group at the same time.
- Great lecturers inspire their listeners.
- Lecturers can predict exactly what will happen during their speech.
- Lecturers believe they are in control.
- Learners do not feel threatened while listening passively.
- Learners know how to listen and take notes.
- Learners do not waste their time sharing their ignorance with each other.
- Learners believe that the lecturer will present correct and critical information.

At the same time, it is easy to create a list of lecture disadvantages:

- Lectures tend to be dull and boring.
- Lectures are pitched too high or too low for different members of the audience.

- Lectures focus on the transfer of information—not on the transfer and application of skills.
- Lectures do not do a good job of transferring information because passively received information is often soon forgotten.
- Lecturers ignore the fact that real learning requires active participation, not passive listening.
- Lecturers tend to focus on what they want to tell the audience rather than on what members of the audience want to know.
- Lecturers do not receive useful feedback.

Interactive Lectures

Interactive lectures facilitate two-way communication. They incorporate highly motivating game elements, yet give complete control to the instructor. Interactive lectures are also flexible; consequently, a trainer can shift between a traditional lecture and the interactive variety with very little effort. If you, as a trainer, know your subject area, you can easily convert the standard lecture into a lecture game.

The issue is not whether trainers should abandon the lecture method, rather, the questions is, how can it be improved? Addressing these three questions can help devise a solution:

1. What elements of the lecture method contribute to its instructional effectiveness?
2. Under what conditions, for which types of students, and for what types of training objectives is the lecture method the most effective?
3. How can we profit from the advantages offered by the lecture method while reducing or removing the disadvantages?

For more than two decades, I have been exploring these questions in various field studies within corporate settings. The result of these studies is a synthesized technique called interactive lectures or lecture games, a powerful new piece of equipment for every trainer's toolbox.

Categories of Interactive Lectures

Seven categories of interactive lecture formats are presented in this book, each with its own particular uses and strengths. There is a wide range of choices that can actually make most lectures more interactive and, ultimately, more effective. Here is a chapter-by-chapter description of each of these interactive lecture methods.

Chapter 2: Active Review and Summary

Adding interactivity to lectures by requiring participants to review what they heard, summarize the key points, and plan the application of the knowledge they gained from the lecture experience is a simple and effective training method. The chapter identifies several ways that participants may review their notes, prepare summaries, work with one another, and share their ideas. Requiring participants to review and summarize lecture content reinforces learning and improves recall.

Chapter 3: Interspersed Tasks

Conducting review and summary activities throughout the lecture rather than leaving them for the end is the basic idea behind the interspersed-tasks approach to interactive lectures. This chapter includes five effective ways to stop your presentation from time to time and conduct an activity that requires participants to review their notes, think back on what they heard, identify key points, relate them to the ideas from previous segments, and share their ideas.

Chapter 4: Integrated Quizzes

Quiz contests provide highly motivating review activities. Instead of sandwiching different learning tasks into your lecture, use different types of quizzes. Stop your presentation from time to time and conduct a quiz activity. After each quiz, discuss errors and misconceptions revealed in participants' responses. Continue your lecture, alternating between lecture and quiz sessions until you have covered the entire training content. This chapter offers four types of quizzes.

Chapter 5: Assessment-Based Learning

Using an assessment-based method, you garner participant involvement up front, before the training session begins. This chapter includes four suitable tests to administer at the beginning of the session. Using the information revealed by participants' responses, you can select appropriate units of your lecture content and arrange them in a suitable sequence to close their knowledge gaps efficiently.

Chapter 6: Participant Control

Instead of conducting expensive and extensive audience analysis prior to the lecture only to find out that this particular audience on the particular day has different needs and preferences, let the participants dictate and control the scope and sequence of the lecture. This chapter includes five ways to encourage one or more participants to tell you what they want to learn and how they want to learn.

Chapter 7: Teamwork

From ancient times, people have figured out that the best way to learn something is to teach it to others. Impressive data from recent experimental research on collaborative learning supports this principle. This chapter includes two top methods for bringing this powerful concept into the classroom—Multilevel Coaching and Team Teaching.

Chapter 8: Debriefing

Debriefing is a systematic approach for encouraging participants to reflect on their experience and share their insights. Failure to conduct a debriefing is the main reason why exciting experiential activities, simulation games, role plays, and outdoor adventures fail to reach their maximum training effectiveness. This chapter gives you a powerful methodology to get value from debriefing.

Wide Use of the Seven Categories

With the exception of debriefing, each of the interactive lecture formats incorporates different formats. Each represents a specific sequence of activities that you can apply to different training topics. For example, the Best Summaries approach (chapter 2) can be used in conjunction with lectures on accounting, banking regulations, customer service, or even zymurgy (a branch of chemistry that deals with the fermentation process). Similarly, by changing the jolt instead of the lecture, you can explore different types of principles and procedures using the Debrief format (chapter 8).

Different categories and formats of interactive lectures share the same basic principle: If you combine the structure and the efficiency of the lecture method with the excitement and participation of interactive strategies, you build a high degree of flexibility into your lectures. You should make use of this feature by

Not too many people know that LECTURE is actually an acronym. It stands for "Lengthy Endless Continuous Torture with Unending Repetition of Explanations."

constantly monitoring participant reactions and switching between the passive-lecture and active-participation modes.

Which Interactive Lecture Format Should You Use?

Your choice of interactive lecture format should depend on your objectives and type of training topics. To simplify this selection process, look at table 1-1. In this table, training topics are categorized into six different domains; the table lists examples of each while identifying the most suitable formats for each domain. This should facilitate your decision about which interactive lecture format to use.

How to Use This Book

This book presents more than two dozen different interactive lectures in a structured-text layout for easy reading and reference.

First you'll see that each interactive lecture technique is highlighted with a special icon to flag the beginning of the relevant section. I've structured these sections in a standard way, making it easy for you to identify the interactive lecture method's key feature, appropriate use, sample topics, handouts, supplies and equipment, preparation, flow of activities, and suitable adjustments. In the section on activity flow, each step is explained using a sample application.

Interactive Lecture Design

For interactive lecture formats that involve handouts, you'll see another icon directing you to its location in the appendix: You may photocopy or modify these handout templates so that they meet your needs and those of your audience.

Handout icon

To show you how the trainer or lecturer interacts with an audience, each exercise in this book offers a detailed explanation of the trainer's role. You can study either the instructions or the examples first, depending on your personal preference.

Number of Participants and Time Requirements

You might have noticed that this book ignores two of the usual elements used in describing training games: number of participants and time requirements. This is because you can conduct interactive lectures with any number of participants and adapt the session to suit any available time. During part of the session, you lecture to the entire group. During the rest of the session, participants work individually, with a partner, or in small teams. Therefore, in either situation, the number of participants is not a critical factor. I have conducted interactive lectures with small groups of four, large groups of 400, and every size in between.

Time requirements for an interactive lecture depend on the length and complexity of your training topic. On one hand, I have compressed the Superlatives session (chapter 2) into a seven-minute presentation followed by a five-minute discussion. On the other hand, I have expanded a Press Conference session (chapter 6) for eight hours (including breaks), allowing participant teams to generate and select questions, as well as listen and summarize answers from five different experts. You, too, can compress and expand any interactive lecture format to suit your topic and your needs.

Feel Free to Experiment

Remember that interactive lectures put you in charge. You can adjust the format to provide the level of interaction that is most comfortable. You must recall, however, that it is not enough to merely cover the topics; it is important to help your students discover the topic. Do not sacrifice the long-term application of principles and procedures for the short-term goal of a rapid data dump.

Enjoy the book!

Table 1-1. Decision table for selecting lecture formats.

Learning Domain	Domain Definition	Sample Topics	Suggested Formats
Informational Domain	Involves technical and factual content	• The information superhighway • The Americans With Disabilities Act • Chemistry of common household cleaners • A brief history of our organization	• Best Summaries • Bingo • Crossword • Essence • Frequently Asked Questions (FAQs) and Fakes • Intelligent Interruptions • Press Conference • Selected Questions • Team Quiz • Thirty-Five • Twos and Threes • Words and Pictures
Procedural Domain	Involves step-by-step activities	• How to deal with senior-citizen customers • Financial planning • Retirement planning • Poster design	• Fishbowl • Item List • Job Aids • Multilevel Coaching • Team Teaching • Thirty-Five
Conceptual Domain	Involves categories, definitions, and examples	• Types of interview questions • Causes of performance problems • Organizational climate variables • Cultural factors	• Brainstorming • Confusion • Egg Hunt • Idea Map • Questionnaire Analysis • Superlatives
Principles Domain	Involves the use of rules and relationships among different concepts	• Sexual discrimination • Soccer rules • Leadership styles • Basic principles of message design	• Idea Map • Item List • Questionnaire Analysis
Interpersonal Domain	Involves concepts, procedures, and principles related to interpersonal interactions	• Impact of management styles • Cross-cultural communication • Methods for conducting a workshop • Ways of handling sexual harassment	• Fishbowl • Questionnaire Analysis • Role Plays • Shouting Match • Items List • Interactive Story
Affective Domain	Involves attitudes, values, and beliefs	• Affirmative action • Gun control • Conflict resolution • Cultural values	• Shouting Match • Interactive Story • Debrief

Active Review and Summary

Adding interactivity to lectures by requiring participants to review what they heard, summarize key points, and plan for action that incorporates the new skills and knowledge gained from the lecture experience is both simple and effective. Participants review their notes, prepare summaries, work with each other, and share their ideas. All of these activities reinforce learning and improve recall. By using an active approach (instead of passively listening to the lecturer rehash the content), the effectiveness of these closing activities is greatly increased.

This chapter offers six methods of implementing active review:

- *Best Summaries:* an activity using index cards to summarize the lecture and vote for the best summary

- *Essence:* a paper-and-pencil exercise that whittles down a 32-word summary to two words
- *Superlatives:* an exercise that lets participants identify the most important elements of a lecture
- *Thirty-Five:* an exercise that allows participants to find the most important point in a lecture
- *Twos and Threes:* participants write questions based on the content of your lecture and then team together to answer them
- *Words and Pictures:* an activity that takes advantage of participants' visual intelligence.

Interactive
Lecture
Design

Best Summaries

Asking listeners to summarize your presentation from time to time is a good technique for encouraging people to listen carefully, take notes, and review the content. This is the basic concept of Best Summaries.

Key Feature

Each participant prepares a summary of the main points at the end of each segment. Teams of participants exchange summaries and select the Best Summary from each set.

When to Use This Format

There are three situations that would make the implementation of Best Summaries ideal. First, this method of active review would be beneficial if the instructional content involves concepts, principles, and procedures. Also, if the lecture experience is formatted so participants are capable of taking notes, summarizing the content, and evaluating other people's summaries, then this active learning method would work. Finally, if you have a logical outline for your presentation, Best Summaries is a good method for an organized lecture.

Sample Topics

These topics are just a few of many to which the Best Summaries method could be applied:

- organizational values
- basic principles of customer service
- doing business in Texas
- the coaching procedure
- life cycle of a high-tech product
- maintaining a database.

Supplies

These three items are both necessary and helpful during the implementation of Best Summaries:

- index cards
- timer
- whistle.

Preparation

Get the aforementioned materials ready before you start this activity. Divide your presentation into logical 10-minute units, and use appropriate flipcharts, slides, or other visual aids to outline the logical flow of your presentation.

Let's walk through an example:

Matt is planning an introductory training session on human performance technology (HPT) for a group of managers. This is how he outlines the content:

1. *Define human performance technology (HPT).*
2. *Describe the analysis step in HPT.*
3. *Explain the design step in HPT.*
4. *Outline the evaluation step in HPT.*
5. *Illustrate the implementation step in HPT.*

Matt thinks that he can cover each topic in 10 minutes. He anticipates spending about 12 minutes for each topic's interactive interlude. Therefore, each topic will require about 22 minutes; he estimates that the whole session will take approximately two hours.

Flow

Brief the Participants at the Beginning of the Lecture. Explain that you will make a series of 10-minute presentations and at the end of each presentation, time will be allotted for each participant to summarize the material presented. Once the summaries have been written, other participants will evaluate the summaries and the Best Summaries will receive special recognition.

Encourage participants to take good notes to help them produce accurate and complete summaries. If the resources are available, announcing that the Best Summaries will be posted on the Internet can often add extra incentive for the participants.

Matt's audience consists of 23 managers, who are all familiar with his unconventional approach to training presentations. As a result, his introductory announcement does not surprise them.

Scheduling. It is important to stick to your schedule. Avoid straying from the time limits you have allotted for various portions of the interactive lecture. If you get too far off track, elements might get rushed or drawn out—either of which will have a negative effect on the lecture experience.

Matt keeps an eye on the clock and sticks to his predetermined schedule. He checks the time frequently to make sure that both the lecture and activity portions of his training experience stay on track.

Present the First Unit. It is now time to start the first unit of the lecture.

After his explanation of the lecture format, Matt presents the first unit. He begins his presentation by identifying the six critical features of HPT (such as its goal-directed nature and the use of different interventions to deal with varying root causes of performance problems). He spends nine minutes on this topic.

Pause for Summaries. At the end of your first lecture topic, distribute blank index cards. Ask participants to summarize your presentation on one side of the card within a set time. Have each participant make up and write a four-digit PIN (player

identification number) on his or her card. Remind the participants that they need to remember this number because they will use them to identify their cards later.

Matt distributes the cards and asks participants to summarize the key items from his presentation in three minutes. He reminds participants to write their PINs on the reverse side of the card.

Form Teams. Organize participants into teams of four to seven members and seat them around a table. Ask one member of each team to collect the summaries and shuffle them.

Matt's participants gather around five tables. To accomplish his goal of having four to seven participants at a table, Matt rearranges the groups so that three tables now accommodate six participants and the fourth table has five. One person from each table then collects and shuffles the index cards.

Exchange and Evaluate. Have the teams exchange stacks of summary cards. One easy way to do this is to give the packet of summary cards from the first team to the second one, the packet from the second team to the third one, and so on, giving the cards from the last team to the first one. Tell the teams to collaboratively review the summaries and select the best one using whatever criteria they want. Be sure to set a suitable time limit that works within your schedule.

Matt picks up the summary cards and redistributes them from one table to the next. He emphasizes that all team members at each table are to participate in the evaluation and discussion of each summary. He announces a three-minute time limit for this part of the activity.

A technical trainer gave his entire presentation in Hindi—and nobody even noticed the difference.

Conclude the Evaluation Activity. At the end of the allotted time, ask each team to read the summary it selected as the best in its pile. After all teams read their Best Summaries, have them read the identification number on the back of the card. Ask this person to stand up and lead a round of applause. Briefly comment on the summaries, identifying the key points and correcting any misconceptions. This is your final opportunity to clear up any confusing points or add a final emphasis on something that might have fallen by the wayside in some of the summaries.

At the end of three minutes, Matt randomly selects the fourth team to read the Best Summary aloud. The rest of the teams follow suit, reading aloud the summary deemed to be the best. After all the teams finish, Matt returns to the fourth team and asks the team to identify the author of the Best Summary using the PIN from the back of the card. He leads a round of applause for Don, the author. Matt then goes around to the rest of the teams who in turn read the PIN and acknowledge the author.

Repeat the Process. Upon completing the evaluation process, settle everyone down for the next unit in your interactive lecture. Follow up with individual summary writing and team evaluation to identify the next set of Best Summaries the same way you did with the first unit.

Matt repeats the same procedure with the other four steps of the HPT process.

Participants write and evaluate the summaries at the end of each round.

Conclude the Session. After the last presentation and evaluation, thank all participants for their contributions to the interactive learning experience. Invite participants to retrieve their summary cards from the table where they were evaluated.

At the end of the session, Matt collects all the Best Summary cards. He promises the participants that he will type up these 20 summaries and post them on a Website. The rest of the summary cards are returned to their authors.

What If...

There Is Not Enough Time? The length of the summaries can be restricted to a single sentence written in a time limit of one minute. Alternatively, you could restructure the lecture experience so as to complete the entire presentation and conduct a single summary round at the end.

There Are Too Many People? Instead of asking all teams to read their Best Summaries, randomly select one or two teams to read their summaries, thus minimizing the amount of time spent sharing but not negating the process of review.

There Are Too Few People? The Best Summaries interactive method works with as few as four participants. Simply organize them into two teams of two members each.

Essence

It takes in-depth understanding to reduce the mysteries of the universe to the five simple characters of $E = mc^2$. Participants do not have to be brilliant scientists to benefit from this activity. However, it does require them to struggle with concepts and principles until they can reduce them to their bare minimum.

Key Feature

After the presentation, ask teams to prepare a 32-word summary and successively reduce it to 16-, eight-, four-, and two-word lengths. At the end of each round, you incorporate main teaching points in the feedback comments.

When to Use This Format

There are two opportune times to use this interactive format. The first of these is when the instructional content contains concepts, principles, and issues rather than facts. The second is when participants have sufficient vocabulary and language skills to write effective summary statements.

Sample Topics

These topics are just a few of many to which the method Essence could be applied:

- special theory of relativity
- employee empowerment
- valuing cultural diversity
- e-commerce
- technologies of the future
- introduction to forensic psychology.

Supplies

Items that are both necessary and helpful during the implementation of Essence include these:

- paper and pencil
- timer
- whistle.

Flow

Brief the Participants. Explain that a team contest will follow your lecture. This will spark competitive drive in many participants, naturally driving them to listen harder and focus more on the lecture portion of the interactive learning experience. After encouraging learners to listen carefully and take notes, start your presentation.

Patti's presentation is about the advantages of online learning. She begins the presentation with the official warning about the follow-up contest. At the end of the presentation, instead of asking for a straight summary, Patti asks the teams to create mission statements for imaginary Web-based learning companies, stressing the advantages of online learning.

Ask for the Initial Summary. Organize participants into approximately equal-sized teams of four to seven members. Tell the teams to come up with summaries that include all the key points in exactly 32 words—no more, no less. Be sure to assign a time limit to this process (five minutes should do it). To write the summary, each team should select a scribe at the beginning of the group work process.

Patti's audience has 32 participants. She organizes them into four teams of five and two teams of six. Howard and Mercedes are on different teams and are both selected by their teams to be the scribes.

Conduct Team Presentations. At the end of five minutes, blow a whistle and ask teams to quickly wrap up their summaries. Then, ask each team to read its statement. Encourage other teams to listen carefully so they can borrow ideas and words from other teams' summaries for later use.

After five minutes, Patti randomly asks the teams to read their 32-word mission statements. This is what Howard reads: "We will radically change the way people learn by providing just-in-time, just-enough, and just-for-me content and activities that continuously and dynamically match the learning, thinking, and personality styles of each individual participant."

Here is the mission statement from Mercedes's team: "We will place online learners in a secure cocoon that provides safety, warmth, nutrition, and encouragement so they can acquire the skills, knowledge, and attitudes needed for a personal transformation and metamorphosis."

Identify the Best Summary. After all teams have completed their presentations, ask individual participants to vote for the summary they feel is best by raising their hands as you point to different teams. Prior to the vote, be sure to announce that participants should not raise their hands more than once or choose their own team's summary. Be sure to congratulate the winning team.

Patti decides to speed up the selection process by acting as a judge and choosing the best statement herself. She selects the statement from one of the teams (not one to which Howard or Mercedes belongs) as the best mission statement. Other teams start to grumble, but Patti briskly moves on. Patti leads a round of applause to congratulate the winner and then moves on to the next part of the activity.

Comment on the Summary Statements. Identify central elements and clarify misconceptions in the summaries. Be sure to

note any elements you felt were important enough to be mentioned in the summaries that might have gone unnoted. Present additional information on important elements if necessary.

Patti justifies her choice of the best mission statement by pointing out that it contains all key advantages of online learning without exaggerating any of them. She then gives examples of wild claims in some of the other mission statements and warns that such statements would disillusion potential users who see them as unachievable.

Shrink to 16 Words. Ask teams to rewrite their summaries in exactly 16 words. Encourage them to borrow ideas from other teams and from your comments. Suggest that teams focus on essential ideas and leave out relatively unimportant ideas, superfluous words, and redundant language. Assign a three-minute time limit.

Upon hearing the announcement and receiving the go-ahead from Patti, the teams go to work. Howard's and Mercedes's teams make suitable adjustments to their original mission statements rather than borrowing from other teams. Here is the 16-word statement from Howard's team: "Use the learner's error rate and response speed to adjust the challenge to a flow state." Mercedes's team comes up with this: "Provide safety, inspiration, nutrition, and encouragement resulting in transformation, growth, wisdom, and the ability to fly."

Repeat the Sharing Procedure. Conduct another round of team presentations of the shortened summaries. Select the best; present your comments and elaborations as needed.

Patti asks team representatives to read their now-shortened mission state-

ments. The winner for this round is Marie's team, which liberally borrowed ideas and words from the other teams.

Shrink to Eight Words. Ask teams to cut the length of their summaries in half—exactly eight words—while retaining the essential ideas. Encourage teams to leave out concepts instead of words. Assign a two-minute time limit.

Howard's team comes up with this eight-word statement: "Personalized learning through automated data collection and adjustment." Mercedes's team builds upon its metamorphosis parallel with this statement: "To provide elements for transforming caterpillars into butterflies."

Final Four. Conduct another round of team presentations and polling. Then ask teams to reduce their summaries to exactly four words by dropping all but essential ideas and tightening up the language. Assign a two-minute time limit.

Unfortunately, neither Howard's nor Mercedes's team wins the eight-word round. Undaunted, they whip out their four-word statements: Howard's team comes up with: "Extreme learning through personalization." And, Mercedes's team continues its metaphor: "Turning caterpillars into butterflies." Patti selects Howard's team's four-word statement as the winner.

It Takes Two. After team presentations and polling, ask teams to reduce their summaries to two words. Assign a one-minute time limit.

The teams rapidly reduce their mission statements to two words. Howard's team comes up with "Personalized learning," and Mercedes's team says,

"Nurturing flight." Patti, however, selects the statement, "Webbest learning" from another team as the two-word winner.

Participants Work Individually. Invite participants to write their own personal summary statement, using as many words as they need. Assign a two-minute time limit for this part of the activity.

The participants work on their individual mission statements. Mercedes writes her version, totally abandoning caterpillars and butterflies. Her no-nonsense mission statement has 20 words: "We will improve the way every person learns by effectively and efficiently matching the learning style of each individual participant."

Conclude the Activity. After two minutes, blow a whistle to end the activity. Ask participants to complete their personal summaries if they have not done so. Thank participants for sharing their perceptions and insights.

What If...

There Is Not Enough Time? Begin with 16-word summaries and end with four-word summaries. This way you can limit the number of rounds used in the activity without ceasing the learning through minimizing summary content. Another method would be to ignore the polling procedure and select the Best Summary for each round yourself (as Patti did) or use a colleague as an external judge.

You Have Lots of Time? Break the presentation into several units and then conduct the Essence activity at the end of each unit. Alternatively, you could ask participants to read their individual statements at the end of the activity if you only wanted to do Essence once.

There Are Too Many Participants? Instead of asking all teams to read their summaries, randomly select two or three to read their summaries. Select the Best Summary from this limited set. During subsequent rounds, select other teams so that everyone has the opportunity to get their ideas expressed during the interactive learning activity.

There Are Too Few Participants? You can make teams with as few as two members or the game can even be played as an individual-participation contest.

Participants Are Already Familiar With the Topic? Use this activity before your presentation. Ask teams to write summary statements that incorporate important concepts, ideas, and issues related to the training topic. Make your presentation while giving feedback on the teams' statements.

Superlatives

One way to ensure effective retention of the lecture content is to encourage participants to review it repeatedly. To keep repetition from becoming boring, subtly change the repeated review task to keep the participants engaged.

Key Feature

After the lecture, ask participants to identify the most important piece of information you presented. After a suitable pause, ask participants to share their decisions. Present another category (such as the most useful or most controversial) and ask participants to select an appropriate point from your presentation that satisfies the requested Superlative. After making the choice, ask participants to pair up with one another and share their choices. Repeat the procedure by identifying different categories and having participants identify a point in your presentation that falls into the respective category.

When to Use This Format

It is recommended that you use this topic when the instructional content contains facts, concepts, principles, and issues. In addition, it is necessary that participants have sufficient skills in taking notes.

Sample Topics

These topics are just a few of many to which the method Superlatives could be applied:

- workplace violence
- project management
- feedback
- time management
- assertiveness
- teamwork.

Supplies

These items are both necessary and helpful during the implementation of Superlatives:

- paper and pencil
- timer
- whistle.

Preparation

Prepare an Outline. Make a list of key topics and steps. These steps can later be used to label key terms and concepts to which Superlatives may be assigned.

Alain's topic is creativity. Here's his outline of steps in the creativity process:

- *Initialize: Recognize an opportunity or problem.*
- *Investigate: Collect relevant facts.*
- *Specify: Identify goals and criteria.*
- *Ideate: Generate ideas.*
- *Iterate: Generate more facts, goals, and ideas.*
- *Incubate: Do something else.*
- *Illuminate: Receive a sudden insight.*
- *Select: Choose the best ideas.*
- *Integrate: Combine ideas into an action plan.*
- *Implement: Apply the action plan.*

Prepare a List of Categories. The idea behind this interactive lecture format is to require participants to identify steps or topics associated with several superlative categories. Make a list of relevant categories before you launch into your presentation. These categories are the superlatives to which participants will assign each key step or idea in your presentation.

Alain prepares this list of categories:

- *most difficult to understand*
- *most popular*

Have you heard about the professor who dreamed he was giving a lecture? He woke up with a start—and found that he really was giving a lecture!

- *most humorous*
- *most controversial*
- *most intriguing*
- *most expensive*
- *most obvious*
- *most subtle*
- *most surprising*
- *most unusual.*

Flow

Brief the Participants. Before your presentation, advise participants to pay careful attention to your lecture and to take ample notes because you will be conducting a review exercise at the conclusion.

Alain encourages the members of the audience to take notes, and he supplies paper and pencil to those who came unprepared.

Make Your Presentation. Do this at a brisk pace and remind participants to take notes because they will come in handy later.

Alain makes a presentation entitled "Ten Steps to Creative Thinking." He identifies each step in the creativity process and briefly describes what happens in each.

Identify a Category and Elicit Responses. After your presentation, ask participants to review the notes and select the most important point in your presentation. After a brief pause, invite others to share points that they consider most important. Question the logic behind various choices made by the participants. This approach forces them to justify their decisions using evidence and other information that you may have presented in your lecture or that they may know from elsewhere. This encourages a sharing and supporting of ideas and information. Add your own comments to support the participants' choices.

Dorothy, one of the participants, checks her notes and decides that the

most important thing is the need for patience. Alain invites John, another participant, to share his choice. According to John, the most important point is the need to keep switching between convergent and divergent thinking styles.

Ask for Alternative Responses. Indicate that there could be more than one correct answer to the question, "Which point is the most important?" Some participants may have identified a different point as being the most important one. Elicit alternative responses from different participants, one at a time. Invite other participants to comment on these choices.

The participants identify seven steps as being the most important! This results in an interesting discussion. Participants challenge and support one another's ideas, and Alain provides comments with additional or supplemental information to enhance the interactivity learning experience.

Identify a New Category. Announce a new Superlative to the group. Give participants a moment to review their notes and reflect upon your lecture so they can identify the point that belongs to this new category.

Alain asks participants to choose the point that is the most different from everything else he talked about. Dorothy decides that it is about the incubation step because it is the only step in which the creative thinker takes on a passive role.

Ask Partners to Discuss Their Choices. Direct participants to find partners. Ask each person in the duo to share his or her point with the other. If both have the same answer, ask them to explain their reasons. If the partners have selected different points, ask them to come to an agreement about which is the most fitting to the superlative being identified.

> *Dorothy pairs up with John who has selected a piece of information about illumination as the most different. They decide that their choices are very similar and that the reason for the choice is the passive nature of the incubation and illumination activities.*

Present Their Choices. After a suitable pause to allow partners to share ideas and express their opinions, select a player at random and ask him or her to announce the most fitting point that the pair came up with. Ask the duo to justify their selection and comment briefly to reinforce their choice. Get other participants to be active in the discussion by offering up their selections as well.

> *Alain selects Mike to share his choice. Mike explains that he and his partner selected the point about the integration step because this requires the creative thinker to combine different ideas rather than generating new ones. Alain calls on a few more groups to discuss their ideas before continuing the lecture experience.*

Identify More Categories. Repeat the procedure with other categories from the list you prepared earlier. Time may not allow for discussion of every superlative you identified during your preparation for the training. This is OK, though. Just do as many as you can to make as much of a rounded learning experience as possible for all the participants.

Conclude the Activity. Congratulate participants for their in-depth analysis and understanding of the lecture content.

What If...

You Do Not Have Enough Time? As previously discussed, the number of superlatives used in this activity can be easily reduced. In addition, you can invite a limited number of people to share their choices and comment on the choices of others according to your time limitations.

You Have Too Much Time? Ask participants to work in teams and discuss each category before selecting a suitable point. Use several different categories.

There Are Too Many Categories? Just use three or four of the most fitting categories. Always start with the most important to the least important so that all of the highlights are hit within the time limit.

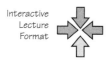

Thirty-Five

A friend of mine recently remarked, "If I paid you a dollar every time I used Thirty-Five, you'd be a rich man now!" Thirty-Five is one of the most versatile training activities that I have designed.

Key Feature
During Thirty-Five, participants reflect on the lecture and identify the most important point, fact, principle, concept, step, or strategy they heard. They write this item on an index card, exchange the card with someone else, and then evaluate one another's cards. The winner in this activity is not the best player, but the best item.

Sample Topics
These topics are just a few of many to which the method Thirty-Five could be applied:

- introduction to Botswana
- marketing strategies
- the coaching process
- negotiation skills
- effective listening
- techniques of technical writing.

Supplies
These things are both necessary and helpful during the implementation of Thirty-Five:

- index cards
- timer
- whistle.

Flow
Brief Participants. After concluding your lecture, distribute index cards to participants. Ask each participant to write a summary sentence that captures an important idea or strategy from the lecture. Instruct participants to keep the item short, specific,

clear, and legible. Set a two-minute time limit for the completion of this task.

Marco completes his lecture on how to start a small business and distributes the index cards. Susan thinks back on the content quickly, reviewing her notes as necessary, and writes this summary sentence: "Prepare a business plan even if you don't plan to present to anyone else."

Let Go. After two minutes, blow the whistle and give instructions for getting ready for the next steps. Ask each participant to review his or her sentence and silently gloat about its elegance and power. Then, ask participants to emotionally detach themselves from their sentence and prepare to launch it into the world.

Susan finds these instructions slightly silly and thinks about changing her summary sentence, but before she can do that, Marco blows the whistle.

Switch Cards. Ask participants to their turn cards down to hide the sentence. When you blow the whistle, ask participants to stand up, walk around, and exchange the cards with each other. Participants should not read the sentences on the cards they receive but should immediately exchange it with someone else. They should continue exchanging cards with one another repeatedly until you blow the whistle again.

Susan exchanges cards about half a dozen times before Marco stops the process.

Find a Partner. After about 20 seconds, blow the whistle again to stop the process.

Ask participants to stop moving and to pair up with any other nearby participant.

When told to pair up, Susan happens to be next to Leslie, so they decided to pair up with one another.

Compare and Score. Ask each pair of participants to review the sentences on the two cards they have. They should distribute 7 points between these two items (no fractions or negative numbers) to reflect their relative merit. Participants should write the number of allotted points on the back of each card, respectively.

Susan's card says: "Keep talking to your customers throughout the planning period," whereas Leslie's card says: "Don't quit your day job." They discuss the importance of these two sentences. They decide to give 5 points to the first card and 2 points to the second.

Conduct the Second Round. After a suitable pause for scoring, blow the whistle again and ask participants to repeat the process of moving around and exchanging cards. Blow the whistle again after around 20 seconds. Like last time, participants should stop moving, find a partner, compare the sentences on their cards, and distribute 7 points. The new set of points should be written below the previous ones.

During the second round, Susan teams up with Ali. They decide to give 6 points to Ron's card with this sentence: Project your sales and profits for the first five years. Susan's card gets a single point for this bland summary sentence: Look before you leap.

Conduct Three More Rounds. Tell participants that you will be conducting three more rounds of the activity. Suggest that participants maintain high levels of objec-

tivity by disregarding earlier numbers and by keeping a poker face if they have to evaluate their own sentence.

Susan works with three other partners, but never runs into the card with her own sentence.

Count Down to the Winning Sentence. At the end of the fifth round, ask participants to return to their seats with the card they currently have. Ask them to add the score points and write the total. After a suitable pause, count down from 35 (the maximum possible). When a participant hears the total on the card, he or she should stand up and read the sentence on the card. Continue this process until you have identified the top five to 10 sentences.

Susan adds up the 5 score points on the back of her card and writes down 26. Much to her surprise, her card turns out to be the one with the third highest total. When she hears 26, she stands up and reads the sentence: "Have alternative strategies for raising the initial capital you need."

Discuss the Items. Briefly comment on the top items and invite participants to make comments.

Marco briefly comments on the similarities and differences among the top-rated cards. He also recalls and reports the highest scoring card from the previous time he conducted this interactive lecture.

Follow Up. Thank participants for generating the summary sentences and evaluating them. Tell them that you will type up a complete set of items and distribute them through email. This email can act as a source of review at any point in the future after the lecture experience.

Being very conscientious, Marco follows up on his promise by sending out the email list the next day.

What If...

There Is Not Enough Time? Conduct just three rounds of pairing and scoring and then begin your scoring countdown at 21 (the new highest possible score). Alternatively, distribute index cards with pre-written summary sentences and ask participants to merely exchange, pair up, and score the cards.

You Have Too Much Time? Conduct the activity several times at the end of each logical unit in your lecture.

You Have an Odd Number of Participants? As you might guess, this happens about half the time. Keep a card with a summary sentence in your pocket. Locate the participant without a partner and pair up with him or her. Compare and score your cards just like other participants. In essence, you become a participant.

One or More of the Cards Is Blank? Have a few prepared cards available. Substitute these cards for the blank cards as necessary.

Twos and Threes

Interactive Lecture Design

Handout available in appendix

One of the most effective approaches for involving participants in the learning process is to ask them to write questions based on the content of your presentation. By asking participants to exchange these questions and then answer them, you double the opportunity for actively processing the information.

Key Feature
The activity consists of three parts. First, participants listen to a lecture, taking careful notes. After the lecture, each participant writes a closed question on a card. For the next several minutes, participants go around the room or table and answer each other's questions, scoring 1 point for each correct answer. After spending several minutes answering closed questions, each participant writes an open question. In the ensuing several minutes, participants gather in three-person groups. Two participants answer each question and the third person assigns points to each response (better responses earning more points).

When to Use This Format
There are three key elements that, when present, create an ideal environment for implementing Twos and Threes. The first of these is when instructional content contains a combination of facts, concepts, and principles. It is also important that the participants are able to recall details of the lecture and have a high-level mastery of the content. Last, it is beneficial to use this method if you have an outline for the presentation.

Handouts
Handouts explaining how to write open and closed questions are very helpful for this interactive learning method. Two examples (handouts 2-1 and 2-2) are provided in the appendix at the end of this book.

Sample Topics
These topics are just a few of many to which the method Twos and Threes could be applied:

- performance improvement strategies
- ways of handling customer complaints
- management strategies
- ideas for motivating employees
- uses of the company intranet
- changes in the sales process.

Supplies
Here are some things that are both necessary and helpful during the implementation of Twos and Threes:

- index cards of two different colors
- timer
- whistle.

Flow
Brief Participants. Announce your training objective and explain that you are going to give a lecture presentation. You should ask participants to listen carefully and take notes because from time to time you will stop the lecture and conduct an interactive interlude that will require everyone to ask and answer questions based on what has been explained so far in the presentation.

Don is conducting a retraining session on industrial safety for 25 employees of a nuclear power plant. He begins his lecture experience by explaining his interactive lecture procedure to the group.

Figure 2-1. Examples of closed and open questions.

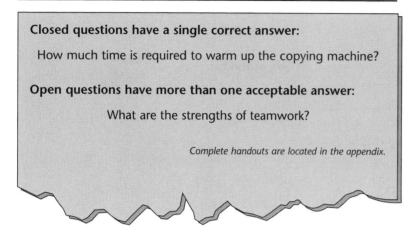

Closed questions have a single correct answer:

How much time is required to warm up the copying machine?

Open questions have more than one acceptable answer:

What are the strengths of teamwork?

Complete handouts are located in the appendix.

Give Your Lecture. Present the first unit of your content. Explain and explore the topic. Do not try anything special; just present accurate and up-to-date information.

> *The first part of Don's lecture is on job-hazard analysis. He identifies the standard method for identifying industrial safety hazards in the workplace. This portion of his lecture lasts 12 minutes.*

Stop Your Presentation. When you have presented enough information to explore the first topic, stop lecturing. It is generally a bad idea to keep talking for more than 15 minutes because minds start to wander and people can't absorb much more information. Feel free to stop abruptly after about 15 minutes even if you have not covered all the information related to the topic.

Announce a Closed Question Interlude. Distribute copies of handout 2-1 about closed questions. Explain that this sheet contains examples of closed questions and quickly demonstrate how to use this task aid. Distribute an index card to all participants and ask them to write a closed question based on the information presented

up to this point in your lecture. Encourage participants to refer to their notes. Announce a two-minute time limit for writing questions.

Explain the Procedure for the Two-Minute Session. At the end of two minutes, blow a whistle and ask participants to get ready for the next activity. Give each participant a blank index card of a different color and identify this as the scorecard. Explain that participants will have three minutes to pair up and exchange questions with as many different participants as possible. In your own words, tell the participants to follow this order of procedures:

1. Stand facing your partner.
2. Decide who will ask the question first.
3. When it is your turn to ask the question, read the question from your card.
4. Wait for the other person to answer.
5. Tell the person if the answer is correct. If it is not, give the correct answer.
6. If the other person's answer is correct, sign your initials on his or her scorecard.
7. When it is your turn to give the answer, listen carefully.
8. Answer immediately. If you do not know the answer, say so.
9. If you gave the correct answer, ask the other person to sign his or her name on your scorecard.
10. Immediately pair up with another participant and repeat the process.

> *Don gives a clear set of instructions, and all the participants are ready to go.*

Conduct the Two-Person Session. Set a timer for three minutes and announce the beginning of the two-person session. Roam around the room and listen in on the questions and answers. (They provide useful feedback about participants' misconceptions.) Blow the whistle at the end of three minutes.

Rick, one of the participants in Don's session, carries a card with this closed question: "What is the first question that you should ask and answer when conducting a job-hazard analysis?" Rick's first partner is Paul who gives the correct answer and gets Rick's initials on the scorecard. Paul's closed question is, "What question should you ask about rotating equipment?" Rick gives the answer: "Will the exposed part of this equipment snag a worker's clothing?" This is a correct answer and, therefore, earns Paul's initials.

Conclude the Two-Person Session. Ask each participant to count the number of initials on the back of his or her card. The number of initials equals the number of points that participant has earned in the round. Tell participants that they will have opportunities to earn more points later. Make a few brief comments about the nature of questions and answers that you overheard, clarifying any misconceptions and emphasizing key points.

During the three-minute period, Rick manages to interact with five participants. He misses only one of the questions and ends up with 4 points during this portion of the activity.

Start the Next Unit. As before, provide accurate, concise content for about seven to 15 minutes.

Don's next segment is on eye and face protection. His presentation lasts for 10 minutes.

Announce an Open Question Interlude. Distribute copies of handout 2-2 for open questions. Explain that this sheet contains examples of open questions and quickly demonstrate how to use this job aid. Distribute an index card to each participant and tell each to write an open question based on the information presented in the preceding part of your lecture. Encourage participants to refer to their notes and then announce a two-minute time limit for writing questions.

Rick finds this task more difficult than writing a closed question. He finally comes up with this two-part question: "Which type of protection can provide the maximum security? Why do you think so?"

Explain the Three-Person Session. At the end of two minutes, blow a whistle and ask participants to get ready for the next activity. Explain that they will have three minutes to form groups of three with as many different participants as possible and exchange their questions. Give the following instructions in your own words:

1. Stand facing the other two members of your three-person group.
2. Decide who will ask the question first.
3. When it is your turn to ask the question, read the question from your card.
4. Ask one of the other people to cover his or her ears.
5. Ask the other person to give his or her answer in a quiet voice.
6. Ask the first person to uncover his or her ears and answer the question.
7. You have 3 points to distribute between the answers from the two different people. You may distribute these points 3-0, 2-1, or 1-2. Sign your initials the appropriate number of times on the scorecards of one or both people.
8. When it is someone else's turn to ask the question, follow the directions.
9. At the end of the round, you would have answered two questions.

Immediately after this round, form a three-person group with two other participants.

Don brings three volunteers to the front of the room and walks them through the procedure, clarifying any confusion that still may exist after he has vocalized instructions.

Conduct the Three-Person Session. Set your timer for three minutes and announce the beginning of the three-person session. Roam around the room and listen in on the questions and answers. Blow the whistle at the end of the set time.

Rick's first group includes Bob and Tom. He likes Tom's answer a little bit better than Bob's. So he signs his initials twice on Tom's scorecard and once on Bob's. In turn, Rick is asked questions by both Bob and Tom, getting two initials for the first and three for the second. He must have really been paying attention.

Conclude the Three-Person Session. Ask each participant to count the number of initials on the back of his or her card and add these points to his or her previous total. Make a few brief comments about the nature of open questions and answers that you overheard.

Rick was able to form three-person groups twice during this interlude. He ended up with a total of 9 points from the four questions he answered.

Continue With Your Lecture. Stop the presentation periodically to conduct additional question-and-answer sessions, alternating between closed and open questions.

Don continues with presentations on three other topics: head protection, electrical safety, and fall protection. Each topic is concluded with either an open or closed question-and-answer session.

Conclude the Session. When you have explored all the topics and conducted the final question-and-answer session, announce the end of your presentation. Often, participants will want to know who had the most points at the end of the interactive lecture; you can figure it out by calling out scores and announcing who had the most initials. Be sure to thank participants for helping you improve the instructional effectiveness of the session.

What If...

There Is Not Enough Time? If possible, divide your training session into two parts. Make longer presentations and shorter interludes. Use two-person (closed-question) interludes only.

There Are Not Enough Participants? Ask each participant to write two closed questions.

You Want to Prepare Your Own Questions? Prepare index cards with closed questions on one side and the answers on the other side. Prepare other cards with open questions and answers. The advantage of using this approach is that you can avoid duplicate and trivial questions. The disadvantage is that you take away useful reflection and review on the part of each participant.

Words and Pictures

If you are familiar with Howard Gardner's book *Frames of Mind: The Theory of Multiple Intelligences* (1993, Basic Books), you will agree that most lectures—including the interactive variety—focus exclusively on linguistic and logical intelligences. Words and Pictures is an interesting format that capitalizes on participants' visual intelligence.

Key Feature

At the end of your lecture, teams of participants prepare two types of summary posters. Some of the posters utilize solely words and the others use only pictures.

When to Use This Format

Two critical contingencies must be fulfilled for Words and Pictures to be a successful interactive method in your lecture experience. First, the instructional content must be clear and suitable for summarizing in graphical form. If the learners are unable to translate into a visual form what you are teaching them, then the activity will not be successful. Second, the participants must be willing to take the risk of testing their graphic skills and visual intelligence.

Sample Topics

The topics listed here are just a few of many to which the method Words and Pictures could be applied:

- performance improvement process
- coaching
- using the flipchart
- production process
- using a videocamera
- organizing a conference.

Supplies

The following things are both necessary and helpful during the implementation of Words and Pictures:

- contest instructions, two different versions
- flipcharts, one per team
- felt-tipped markers
- timer
- whistle.

Flow

Brief Participants. At the beginning of your presentation, encourage participants to listen carefully and take notes because there will be a contest at the end. After encouraging good note taking, proceed with your presentation.

> *Brian is conducting a training session on high-performance teamwork with employees from a pharmaceutical company. He begins the session by telling participants to get ready for the contest at the end.*

Organize Teams. After your presentation, organize participants into four teams so that each team has two to six players. (If you have more than 24 participants, organize them into six teams.) For the activity to work, there must be an even number of teams. It does not matter if a team has one more person or one fewer person than the others. Ask each team to stand around a flipchart.

> *Brian's audience has 37 members, so he sets up eight teams. Five of the teams have five members each and the*

other three have four. Team members station themselves around one of the eight flipcharts located in the room.

Give Instructions to the Teams. Distribute handout 2-3 to two of the teams (Words-Only teams). If you have six teams, give the instructions to three of the teams. Give handout 2-4 to the two or three other teams (Pictures-Only teams).

Handout available in appendix

Tell the team members to read their instructions carefully and then answer any questions that they may have. Be sure to emphasize the five-minute time restriction given to both groups.

Brian gives half of the teams the Words-Only instructions and the other half the Pictures-Only instructions.

Begin the Activity. Start your timer and blow the whistle to indicate the beginning of the poster activity. Keep announcing the remaining time at the end of each minute so teams can pace themselves accordingly.

Brian floats around the room watching the teams in action. He discovers that the teams are going to require more than five minutes. He announces an extension of the time to seven minutes.

Conclude the Activity. After five minutes (or more depending on how the activity went in your setting), blow the whistle again to indicate the end of the time limit.

Compare the Posters. Place the Words-Only posters side by side. Invite all participants from the Pictures-Only teams to study the posters. After a minute, ask participants to indicate their preference by raising their hands or by applauding as you point to each poster in turn. Repeat the same procedure with the Pictures-Only posters by polling members of the Words-Only teams.

Brian provides pieces of masking tape to the Words-Only team members and asks them to mount their four posters on the wall. He gives each individual member of the other teams a colored dot to place on the poster he or she prefers. After the voting, Brian asks the Pictures-Only teams to mount their posters on the opposite wall. He repeats the colored-dot polling procedure.

Combine the Posters. Prompt the participants to return to their original seats. Place all the posters in the front of the room, and conduct a brief discussion on how to use the elements from all posters to create a single poster. This is a good way to summarize the key points from your lecture and leave a concluding, unified impression on your learners.

What If...

There Is Not Enough Time? Limit the Words-Only teams to a single sentence and the Pictures-Only teams to a single icon.

You Have Too Much Time? Break the presentation up into several parts. Conduct Words and Pictures at the end of each part. Also, ask all teams to prepare a combined Words-and-Pictures poster at the end.

There Are Too Many Participants? This should not present a major problem as long as you divide them into an even number of teams. Instead of setting up a flipchart for each team, place a sheet of flipchart paper on different tables for the teams to use to minimize supplies necessary for the activity.

There Are Too Few Participants? You can conduct this activity with as few as eight participants and still use teams. If you have only four participants, conduct the activity as a contest among individuals.

Concluding Thoughts

Here are some notes from the field about interactive lectures that involve active review and summary:

- From the participants' point of view, the most engaging format is Thirty-Five. Participants enjoy walking around, mingling with others, partnering with different people, and engaging in heavy discussions. Words and Pictures is another engaging format.

- From the facilitator's point of view, Superlatives is the easiest format to conduct because you can come up suitable adjectives on the spot. Twos and Threes is perhaps the most challenging format because the mechanics are somewhat complicated.

- The effectiveness of Best Summaries depends on the open-ended questions incorporated in the activity. Invest time in crafting comprehensive and thought-provoking questions. In contrast, Essence produces effective results without the facilitator having to come up with special questions.

- For interactive lecture formats based on active review and summary, you complete your lecture presentation before conducting an activity to help your participants review and summarize the key points. Because all the action takes place at the end of the lecture, your participants may be tempted to take a nap during the earlier phase of passively listening to your lecture. To reduce this unfortunate possibility, you might have come up with the brilliant idea of stopping your lecture at frequent intervals and conducting suitable activities during the lecture.

That's the basic idea behind the category of interactive lectures explored in the next chapter.

Interspersed Tasks

Conducting review and summary activities throughout the lecture rather than waiting until the end is the basic idea behind the interspersed-tasks approach to interactive lectures. During these summary or review activities, you interrupt the presentation occasionally to conduct an activity that requires participants to review their notes, think back on what they heard, identify important points, relate them to the ideas from the previous segment, or share their ideas. After each interlude, be sure to return to your lecture so as to maintain the focus on the big picture. Whenever appropriate, use the key points from the preceding activity as a springboard for your continuing presentation.

This chapter offers five methods for summarizing previous key points and then making a transition to the next portion of your lecture:

- *Idea Map:* encourages the use of an Idea Map to take better notes and increase learning
- *Intelligent Interruptions:* encourages participants to interrupt your lecture though the use of a card deck
- *Interactive Story:* presenting a case study in the form of a story and allowing participants to help tell and solve the problems in the story
- *Job Aids:* using a Job Aid as the basis for your lecture
- *Role Plays:* a lecture game that will allow you to use role playing without fear of losing control.

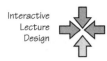

Idea Map

When participants take good notes, learning effectiveness increases significantly. Idea Mapping uses this principle.

Key Feature

During your presentation, participants take notes using an Idea-Mapping approach. At logical junctures, you stop the presentation and ask teams to consolidate their Idea Maps into a combined product. At the end of the lecture, teams complete their Idea Maps, covering the entire presentation.

When to Use This Format

There are several times when using Idea Maps would prove the most beneficial. These include

- when the instructional content is primarily informational or conceptual
- if participants are capable of using the Idea Map approach for taking notes and are capable of working in teams
- whenever you can use the Idea Map to outline your presentation.

Sample Topics

Handout available in appendix

Topics for which Idea Maps would be ideal include, but are certainly not limited to, the following:

- the changing face of Eastern Europe
- chemistry of common household cleaners
- financial planning
- the future of mobile computing
- major concepts of the Hindu religion
- quality management.

Handouts

If you are using Idea Maps for connecting your lecture segments to make clear, easy-to-understand segues, you should give each participant a copy of the outline you are following. Wait until the end of the lecture to distribute the handouts as study aids. That way, the participants will feel more inclined to listen during the lecture.

Equipment and Supplies

The following supplies will facilitate your Idea-Map–based interactive lecture:

- media equipment needed for your presentation
- flipchart
- markers.

Flow

Explain What the Group Will Be Doing. The first thing you should do is introduce the topic and format. Do this by outlining your presentation topic and explaining to the participants that they will take notes using an Idea-Mapping approach. From time to time, during a pause in the presentation, participants get together in teams and create a joint Idea Map of the content covered thus far in the presentation. Handout 3-1 (in the appendix) offers some ideas about how to get started with Idea Mapping.

Jafari introduces the concept of working at home via electronic equipment. He briefly explains the Idea-Mapping procedure and the fact that the group will be using this technique to enhance their recall of his presentation.

Make the First Unit of Presentation. Now you should initiate your presentation by

Figure 3-1. Example of Idea Mapping.

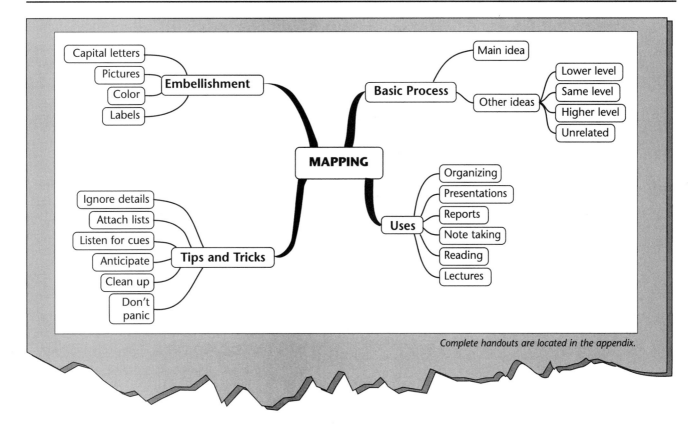

Complete handouts are located in the appendix.

going over the first subject you want to cover. This unit should take between seven and 12 minutes. Stop your presentation at some logical point within that timeframe.

Jafari's presentation begins with a definition of working at home and a list of its advantages and disadvantages. He discusses these topics and explains them by using several examples, pausing after about 12 minutes.

Organize Teams and Start Idea Mapping. Have participants organize into teams. Ask them to spend the next five minutes collaboratively drawing an Idea Map of the topics covered so far. While the teams are busy mapping, walk around listening to their conversations and observing their products to get indirect feedback on the organization of your lecture. You can often

determine whether or not your presentation is clearly organized if the participants are able to develop cohesive Idea Maps.

Jafari asks the participants to form groups of four to six. He then distributes sheets of flipchart paper to each team and asks them to combine their notes into a single Idea Map using colored, felt-tipped pens. While the teams are busy with their task, Jafari takes a quick glance at his Idea Map outline to get ready for the next unit of the presentation. He then observes the teams in action.

Continue With the Presentation. Begin by commenting on any misconceptions or insights you might have heard or observed while watching the participants develop their Idea Maps. Once any issues have been cleared up or key points further emphasized, move on to the next instructional topic.

Jafari reports that most teams found it easier to recall the advantages of working at home rather than the disadvantages; he believes that he should briefly review the major disadvantages. After that, he proceeds to the topic of equipping the home office with various high-tech devices. Following this, he talks briefly about the legal aspects of working at home.

Repeat the Idea-Mapping Interludes. At appropriate junctures, stop the presentation and have teams get together and expand their Idea Maps to cover the recent topics. Repeat this process as often as time permits.

Conclude the Presentation. When all of your lecturing segments have been discussed and the groups have mapped out the key ideas and features in each segment, ask teams to complete their Idea Maps.

Jafari's presentation ends with a set of suggestions on how independent workers can use email to compensate for the absence of conversations around the water cooler. The teams return to complete their Idea Maps with high-tech strategies for socialization.

Facilitate a Show-and-Tell Session. After teams have completed their Idea Maps, have them display the final products. Encourage participants to review other teams' products and compare them with their own. Encourage them to think about ideas they might have left out or things they thought other teams should have included.

The teams attach their Idea Maps to the wall with masking tape. Along with the other participants, Jafari reviews the different Idea Maps.

Comment on the Idea Maps. After the review of different Idea Maps, reassemble the participants. Talk about the common themes among different maps. Identify any missing points and correct any misconceptions that teams might have had. If you find one misconception to be very prevalent, you may want to spend time emphasizing and clarifying that key point.

Jafari comments on the similarity in the way most teams organized the content. He also tells participants that they should pay a bit more attention to the legal aspects of working at home because this element seems to have the least detail in the maps.

Distribute Your Complete Idea-Map Handout. When the participants have the handout, suggest that they compare it with their own individual Idea Maps to see if there are major differences.

Jafari distributes his Idea Map and suggests that participants do the comparison as homework because he is out of time.

What If...

There Is Not Enough Time? Eliminate all Idea-Mapping interludes except the final one. Assign a specific time limit for creating the Idea Map all at once. Stop the activity at the end of this time limit even if participants have not completed the maps.

Participants Do Not Know How to Create Idea Maps? Introduce Idea Maps using the instructions given in this chapter and the handout provided in the appendix in this chapter. Alternatively, conduct a demonstration lesson on Idea Mapping techniques prior to your interactive lecture. When you assemble the teams, make sure each team includes one or two people who know how to do Idea Mapping and can quickly relate the concept to the other members of their team.

There Are Too Few or Too Many Participants? If there are too few participants, instead of having teams of four or five members, ask participants to pair up and collaborate on an Idea Map. If there are too many, then you can make groups larger than four or five people. In short, adjust group size as necessary.

The Final Idea Map Reveals Major Misconceptions? Be happy you found out now while you're still in contact with all of the participants. To remedy this situation, you can either do an additional lecture unit to straighten out the misconceptions or you can prepare and distribute a handout to clarify the concept.

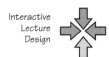

Interactive
Lecture
Design

Intelligent Interruptions

According to communication scientists, the ability to be interrupted is a key feature of interactivity. When you are talking with a bunch of friends, everyone interrupts everyone else; these natural interruptions do not impede whatsoever the conversation at hand. When you are making an instructional presentation, however, most participants will not interrupt you—even if you invite them to do so. This reluctance is due to a combination of politeness, fear of attacks by the presenter, and anxiety about ridicule from the other participants. In Intelligent Interruptions, participants are forced to interrupt you, which helps to make the lecture interactive and more like a daily conversation.

Handout
available in
appendix

Key Feature

You stop your presentation at random intervals and select a participant to interrupt you. This participant is required to ask questions, make comments, or challenge your statements.

When to Use This Format

Ideal situations to use the Intelligent Interruptions approach to interactive learning include when:

- The instructional content is informational.
- Participants are capable of asking appropriate questions and making appropriate comments.
- You can listen to interruptions, react appropriately, and return to your presentation.

Sample Topics

Among the topics that are appropriate for this learning tool are the following:

- business partnership in Canada
- giant magneto-resistance (GMR) technology
- how to watch a soccer game
- information highway
- the Midwest's role in the global economy
- retirement planning.

Handouts

It's recommended that you develop a handout that supplements your presentation to provide something that the participants can use to follow along. Handout 3-2 offers some ideas for Intelligent Interruptions. In addition, it's a good idea to provide a list of appropriate interruptions that can facilitate the activity.

Supplies and Equipment

The following items will be useful when performing this kind of activity:

- two decks of playing cards arranged in the same order
- timer.

Flow

Distribute Cards. When participants arrive, give each person a playing card from the top of one of the decks. After the last person has received his or her card, take the same number of cards from the top of the other deck. Shuffle these cards, which are the duplicates of the cards you distributed to participants, and place the shuffled cards at a location convenient to where you'll be lecturing.

Pierre's session is on workplace violence. He brings two new decks of cards to the presentation and distributes cards from one of them. Just before starting his presentation, he checks the deck and sees the four of diamonds on top. He takes all the cards up to the four of diamonds from the second deck and shuffles the packet of cards matching those he handed out.

Brief Participants. Start the session by distributing the handout 3-2 that lists the types of interruptions and briefly explains each type. Announce that when the timer goes off, you will stop your presentation and pause 30 seconds for everyone to get ready to make an Intelligent Interruption. At the end of the 30 seconds, pick a card and announce its value. Require the participant who has the matching card to make one of the several different types of interruptions that he or she should now have prepared.

Pierre distributes the handout and briefly explains how each type of interruption works.

Set a Timer. Without letting any participants see the time, set your timer for a random period between three and 10 minutes.

Pierre sets his timer for four minutes and 27 seconds.

Begin Your Presentation. Make the presentation in your usual style.

Pierre begins with a horror story from a recent news item to illustrate the effect of violence in the workplace. He emphasizes that by the time violent acts occur, it is too late to do anything about them. He stresses the importance of preventing violence in the workplace by removing the causes and opportunities.

Stop the Presentation. When the timer goes off, stop speaking even if you're in the middle of a sentence. It's time to pause for your first Intelligent Interruption.

Figure 3-2. Example of Intelligent Interruptions.

1. **Apply**
2. **Disagree**
3. **Illustrate**
4. **Paraphrase**
5. **Personalize**
6. **Question**

Complete handouts are located in the appendix.

When the timer goes off, Pierre is explaining the behavioral characteristics of potentially violent employees. He is cut off mid-sentence: "They often co . . . "

Pause While Participants Prepare. Announce a 30-second preparation time. Participants should select any type of interruption from the list and prepare an interruption, following the guidelines, that relates to what has been discussed in the lecture. Encourage them to review their notes and think back on the main points in the presentation.

Pierre observes interesting behaviors among the participants. John closes his eyes and appears to be meditating. Steve begins mumbling to himself. Madhu pulls out different colored highlighters and attacks her notes. Laura and Rob are in a whispered conversation; Pierre decides not to force them to work independently.

Select a Participant. Shuffle your stack of cards, pick one, and announce its value. Ask the person with the matching card to stand up and make the interruption.

Pierre picks the two of clubs. Mike groans and then paraphrases Pierre's presentation. He informs everyone that the key element in handling workplace

Dr. Ellison's Rating Scale for the Objective Measurement of Boredom:

1. Spending a sleepless night counting imaginary sheep.
2. Watching the same B-movie for the 18th time.
3. Counting the number of jelly beans in a gallon jar.
4. Working on an assembly line, tightening a nut every 17 seconds.
5. Listening to a PowerPoint presentation on a technical topic.

violence is to be prepared for all contingencies. Among other things, this involves identifying potential attackers and their targets. Unfortunately, however, this process may violate individual employees' right to privacy.

React to the Interruption. When the participant has finished giving his Intelligent Interruption, give feedback on the accuracy and appropriateness of what was said and how. Respond to any questions and provide a nondefensive rebuttal to any criticism. Always reinforce the participant's efforts.

It takes a special skill to speak for any length at a single pitch and tone. Yet, many lecturers are highly accomplished at this art.

Pierre says that the paraphrase was accurate and commends Mike for intelligently highlighting the most important points. He suggests that he would prefer to use the term tradeoff instead of violation in connection with individual employees' right to privacy.

Repeat the Procedure. Set the timer for another random interval. Continue your presentation and stop again when the timer goes off. Pause for preparation, listen to the interruption, and respond appropriately.

Pierre sets the timer for 10 minutes and 10 seconds. He continues with his presentation, discussing strategies for preventing employees and customers from bringing weapons to the workplace. He stops in the middle of comparing alternative strategies when the timer goes off, and he selects Susan to interrupt. She decides to debate the issue. She argues that the strategies suggested by Pierre will drastically reduce the level of trust among the employees and make them paranoid. This will reduce productivity in the workplace. In his response, Pierre agrees with Susan's point but claims that this is one of the costs of making the workplace safe for everyone. Such

safety will increase trust levels in the long run.

Modification. To keep participants alert, change the procedure from time to time. For example, ask that each participant work with a partner in preparing for the next interruption. These small alterations keep Intelligent Interruptions from becoming mundane.

During the next interruption, Russ asks a series of questions. Instead of responding to these questions, Pierre announces another 30-second pause during which participants are to prepare answers for Russ's questions. He then picks up the five of clubs and thus selects Angela to give her answers to Russ's questions.

Conclude the Presentation. When you finish the session, conduct a final round of interruptions. This time, however, tell participants that any volunteer can present any type of interruption but will not have the 30-second preparation time.

John volunteers to paraphrase the last segment. Next, Vicki applies the content of the entire presentation by describing an action plan to protect herself from workplace violence.

What If...

There Is Not Enough Time? You can make the activity shorter through a variety of methods. First, you can reduce the number of interruptions. If you tell the participants they must use one specific type of interruption, such as the paraphrase, you can reduce preparation time or you could not pause for preparation at all. When the timer goes off, if you immediately pick a card to select a random participant, then activity time will be greatly reduced.

There Are Too Many Participants? Ask the selected participant to speak loudly enough so that everyone can hear. Alternatively, ask the participant to come to the front of the room.

The Interruption Indicates a Misunderstanding? Do not make fun of the participant; instead, use this information as valuable feedback. Question a couple of other participants to determine if this misunderstanding is widespread and clarify if necessary.

Interactive Story

Good storytellers make effective trainers. In the Interactive Story format, participants listen to your story and decide what happened, why it happened, or what should happen next.

Key Features

You present a case incident in the form of a story, pausing at critical junctures in the story. During the pause, let participants decide the cause of a problem or the appropriate strategy for devising and implementing a solution.

When to Use This Format

Certain types of interactive lecture situations optimize the benefits of Interactive Story. These include, but are certainly not limited to:

- The instructional content requires the analysis of a situation, identification of the basic cause, or selection of the best solution.
- Participants have enough experience or expertise in this type of decision making.
- You can present the case incident in the form of a story.

Sample Cases and Decisions

Listed below are some examples of questions you can impose on your participants that prompt their decision making:

- *Conflict incidents:* What strategy should we use?
- *Cross-gender interactions:* How offensive is the man's behavior to a woman?
- *Managerial behaviors:* What is the likely impact?
- *Performance problem anecdotes:* What is the major cause?

- *Sales scenarios:* What is the next step?
- *Stories about customer complaints:* Which expectation is unmet?

Handouts

This activity doesn't *require* any handouts; however, you may find it beneficial to distribute a checklist to help participants analyze the case incidents and organize key facts.

Flow

Prepare for the Presentation. To set yourself up for the presentation, you need to create or obtain a set of case incidents and revise each case so that it encourages systematic analysis. Having made the aforementioned revisions, outline the story and specify the starting point and the ending point in a clear manner.

> *John's session is on cultural differences. He wants to illustrate how people of other cultures differ in their perception of time, gender roles, status, teamwork, and personal achievement. His first story deals with the respect for age in Asian cultures. He prepares an outline for this story based on the actual experience of a colleague.*

Brief Participants. Explain the experience of the interactive format to the participants so they know what's coming. You should organize them into teams that make sense for the size of the group you have at your lecture.

> *John asks the 18 participants to split up into three teams. He explains that he will tell a series of stories to help them recognize how cultural differences affect cross-cultural productivity.*

He tells participants to listen carefully because he will stop at a critical juncture and ask them to analyze some aspect of the story in relation to cultural differences.

Narrate the First Story. Now you're at the stage where you should start telling your first story. Be sure to make it interesting and supply details so that the listeners have to separate the critical information from irrelevant data.

John's story is about Kevin, a total quality management (TQM) trainer who consults with a factory in South India. Kevin has convinced his counterparts to replace the traditional lecture with interactive presentations. The local trainers accept the idea and create outlines for interactive lectures.

One day, the retired founder of the corporation visits the group. During a rambling speech, he says that Kevin is a guru and an embodiment of the goddess of knowledge. Much to Kevin's dismay, most of the trainees agree with the retired founder. To prevent major damage, Kevin interrupts the founder and explains that recent findings in cognitive science have demonstrated the benefits of encouraging the students to challenge the trainer's statements. The elderly man ignores Kevin and insists that humility is the most important requirement for a good student. Several trainers agree. Soon after this incident, the project is canceled for some spurious reason and Kevin is sent back to the United States.

Specify the Task for the Group. Now, you should choose some element in the story about which participants will have to make a decision. Explain that the group should discuss the story and collaborate

on making a decision to answer the question with which you have presented them. Be sure to announce a time limit for this part of the exercise.

John asks the teams to review their notes and to identify the most probable cause for the cancellation of the project. After five minutes' discussion, he wants a representative of each team to report the decision made by the group and justify its conclusion.

Provide Additional Information. Halfway through the teams' discussions, announce that you will answer one or two questions from each team to clarify the story. Limit the questions to the content of the story. Make up appropriate details for your response, but stay within the constraints of the case incident. This approach gives the teams the opportunity to identify the most important issues, clarify them with whatever extra information you give them, and then proceed to the most logical decision. All of these are vital elements in decision making, and they encourage interactivity.

The first team wants to know if any of the trainers in Kevin's group were women. John says, "No." The next team wants to know if Kevin had personality conflicts with his trainers. John explains that Ram, a trainer, disagreed frequently with Kevin but agreed with the importance of student interaction. John answers a few more questions and asks the teams to continue their discussions.

Ask for Reports. Instruct each team to give its conclusion and to justify it. Comment on the teams' conclusions, and present your own conclusion, along with a justification.

The first team suggests that the enormous difference between interactive lectures and traditional lectures caused the problem. The second team suggests that the trainers always disagreed with Kevin but did not want to confront him. The third team suggests that Kevin showed disrespect to the founder of the organization and, therefore, insulted all the employees. In his comments, John reminds the participants that the factory had adopted several TQM approaches that were radically different from the traditional procedures. John also recalls that Kevin's trainers had created interactive lecture outlines and enjoyed the process. John suggests that respect for age is the most probable cause of Kevin's problems because in many cultures, it is very rude to argue with elderly people, who are considered wise by virtue of their age.

Review the Session. After repeating the Interactive Story method a few times to break up the duration of your lecture, summarize the major points. Invite participants to ask questions about the topic you've been discussing and, time permitting, they may even be able to relate some personal stories.

John summarizes his session by identifying five major cultural variables (respect for age, gender role assignments, respect for the teacher, power distance, and need for structure). During the question-and-answer session,

some participants want to know to what extent these cultural differences are present within U.S. organizations. John explains that similar value conflicts frequently arise among American workers who belong to different ethnic groups.

What If...

There Is Not Enough Time? Make your stories more succinct and use fewer of them. Also, the amount of time granted for team discussions may be reduced as necessary.

Participants Lack the Necessary Expertise? Introduce the appropriate principles and procedures before using this interactive lecture format.

Team Discussions Reveal Misconceptions About the Main Idea? If this is the case, stop the discussions and give them a menu of alternative conclusions from which to choose. Ask the teams to discuss each conclusion and to justify rejecting or selecting it.

All Teams Arrive at Incorrect Conclusions? This provides an excellent opportunity for correcting misconceptions and dispelling prejudices.

Teams Strongly Justify Incorrect Conclusions? In addition to correcting misconceptions, revise the story to strongly direct the participants' attention toward the relevant cues.

Interactive
Lecture
Design

Job Aids

Checklists, decision tables, glossaries, recipes, and worksheets are examples of Job Aids that improve people's performance. This game uses a Job Aid as the basis for the presentation.

Key Feature
Participants observe a presentation on the use of a Job Aid. They then use the Job Aid, initially in teams and afterward on an individual basis. To give you an idea of what a Job Aid is, here are a few useful examples:

- worksheet for computing the appropriate price for a new product
- chart of symbols for copyediting a manuscript
- flowchart for selecting the best instructional method for a particular topic
- decision table for selecting the best solution for a specific problem
- checklist for creatively solving a problem
- annotated diagram for troubleshooting a computer.

When to Use This Game
As a trainer, you will find Job Aids most beneficial in the following situations, in addition to many others:

- The instructional content involves a procedure.
- Participants are capable of working individually and in groups.
- You have a Job Aid and several application exercises.

Handouts
To facilitate the learning process during your interactive lecture, you should hand out an appropriate Job Aid for the participants to study and use as they see fit. Also, you should provide a handout of application exercises that would demonstrate when the use of a Job Aid is appropriate. Give an overview of how the Job Aid is applied and explain its format. Ask the participants to look over the Job Aid.

Flow
Prepare the Materials. Select your Job Aid and make copies for your participants. Prepare several application exercises.

Aida's presentation is on using plain, simple English to communicate with non-native speakers. She develops the Job Aid depicted in handout 3-3.

Aida distributes the checklist and asks participants to rapidly review it. She explains that the guidelines are independent of each other; they need not be applied in the order in which they are printed.

Handout available in appendix

Present the First Application Exercise. Set up the context in which a Job Aid might be used and display the item on an overhead screen or distribute handouts.

Aida distributes copies of a paragraph from the employee handbook as an example of inappropriate English to use with non-native speakers. She explains that she will demonstrate how to apply her Job Aid to simplify the paragraph.

Apply the Job Aid. Walk through the use of the Job Aid, eliciting as many suggestions from participants as possible.

Aida asks the group to study the paragraph and to suggest ways to clarify it.

David points out that the paragraph uses complicated, lengthy words in violation of the first guideline. Aida agrees and asks participants for simpler substitutes. Maria suggests that the term "monthly compensation" be replaced by "paycheck." Jacob suggests that "the employee" can be replaced by the pronoun "you." Ulrich suggests treating "overtime" and some other words as technical terms that should be defined. Aida incorporates these suggestions and rewrites the paragraph.

Encourage Everyone's Participation. To make the learning experience as effective as possible, you should do two things. First, call on particular participants by name and ask for their suggestions. Also, you should avoid giving too many suggestions yourself because they can detract from the participants' learning experience.

Aida asks Linda for her ideas, prompting her to identify sentences that could be changed to the active voice.

Unused Job Aid Items. Some of the items in the Job Aid may not be applicable to the exercise. If so, identify these items and comment on them. You can explain why they were not appropriate for the exercise you were doing, and give situations in which they would prove to be beneficial.

Aida points out that the guideline on the use of visuals is not applicable to this paragraph. However, she explains that a diagram may be useful in describing the organizational hierarchy in another section of the handbook.

Team Job Aid Application. Divide participants into teams and give the teams a new application exercise. Have them work on the exercise, applying items in the Job Aid when appropriate.

Aida gives the participants double-spaced copies of another paragraph from the same handbook. She has eight participants in her workshop, and she suggests that everyone work with a partner. She asks the participants to use the checklist to rewrite the paragraph. She encourages the partners to discuss each guideline and its application. While the partners work, Aida walks around, providing help and examples.

Individual Job Aid Application. Upon completion of the teamwork phase in the interactive lecture, dissolve the teams. Give participants a new application exercise for independent work. They should follow the same methodology in regard to Job Aid application, but this time they are testing their ability to do it independently.

Aida hands out a third paragraph; she asks participants to work individually to simplify it. She walks around, talking to different participants and answering their questions.

Conclude With a Question-and-Answer Session. When the participants are done with their individual Job Aid activity, invite them to ask you questions. Respond to them and ask questions of them to make sure that they have mastered the use of the aid.

What If...

There Is Not Enough Time? If minimal time is available, do a quick walkthrough of Job Aid application without too much audience participation. Assign the application exercises as homework.

The Job Aid Is Very Complex? Divide it into two or more parts and walk participants through the first part. Follow up with team and individual exercises. Now repeat the same procedure with the other parts.

Participants Do Not Have Prerequisite Skills or Knowledge? During the initial walkthrough, explain the basic terminology and concepts. Another option is to deal with the prerequisites in a separate training session.

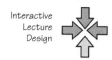

Role Play

Despite its obvious effectiveness in helping participants achieve interpersonal skills, many instructors are reluctant to use Role Play because they fear they will lose control of their session. The following lecture game may help you use Role Play without having this happen.

Key Feature

The presenter conducts a spontaneous Role Play to illustrate interpersonal concepts and skills.

When to Use This Game

Role Play is most effective in specific situations. These situations include, but are certainly not limited to, when:

- The instructional content involves interpersonal concepts, such as types of defensive behavior, or interpersonal procedures, such as active listening.
- Participants are capable of taking part in unrehearsed Role Play.
- You are capable of guiding the Role Play and handling unanticipated events.

Sample Topics

Certain topics for which Role Play may enhance learner's recall include

- active listening
- confronting a disruptive team member
- dealing with a discriminatory remark
- handling unwanted sexual advances
- listening to customer complaints
- marriage counseling.

Handout available in appendix

Handouts

You should hand out a glossary that lists and defines interpersonal concepts, or a checklist that identifies the steps in the interpersonal procedure that goes along with your lecture subject.

Flow

Introduce the Topic. Identify the interpersonal concepts or procedures and explain the topic briefly.

> *Kevin is conducting a session on nondefensive listening. He begins by briefly explaining the topic and emphasizing its importance. This type of active listening is essential between a manager and an employee, between an employee and a customer, between a wife and a husband, and among team members.*

Distribute the Handouts. Each participant should be given a copy of the handout designed to go with your interactive lecture. If your session is about interpersonal concepts, use a glossary. A checklist with step-by-step instructions can be beneficial if your session is about an interpersonal skill.

> *Kevin distributes copies of a glossary (handout 3-4 in the appendix). This glossary lists and defines seven terms describing defensive behaviors and eight terms describing nondefensive behaviors. Kevin explains that all of these behaviors occur in response to remarks or complaints from another person. Kevin specifies that the session will deal with handling legitimate complaints.*

Conduct the Initial Role Play. Set up the Role Play by describing an interpersonal situation. Identify the role you are going to play. Ask a volunteer to play the other role, assuring participants that all this person has to do is to behave naturally. Advise the volunteer not to try anything too dramatic.

> *Kevin narrates a scenario: He and one of his colleagues were asked to prepare the final report on a project they had completed. They decided to divide the report into two sections. Kevin was to write one of them and his colleague, the other. They agreed to meet every day and trade what they had written. Kevin, however, skipped the first two meetings because his daughter was sick. He had also been suffering from writer's block. This is the third day, and Kevin turns up at the meeting without anything written.*
>
> *Following Kevin's presentation, Mary volunteers to be the colleague who has done her share of the work. She is ready to Role Play a confrontation with Kevin.*

Conduct the Role Play. Portray the concepts or procedural steps without acting in an unnatural way. Make sure that the volunteer does not get carried away.

> *Mary has no difficulty playing a frustrated colleague and jumps right in with an attack. She points out that Kevin has betrayed her by not doing his share of the work and not keeping her informed. Kevin tries to explain that his daughter is very sick. He accepts blame for not having informed Mary, but he believes that several things beyond his control prevented him from working on the report. He points out that during the previous month Mary was late with one her proposals.*

Figure 3-3. Example of glossary used during Role Play.

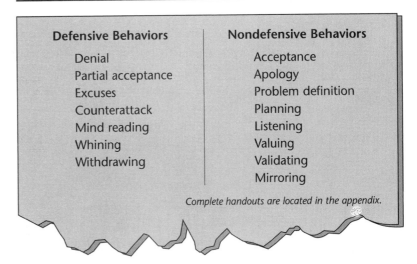

Defensive Behaviors	Nondefensive Behaviors
Denial	Acceptance
Partial acceptance	Apology
Excuses	Problem definition
Counterattack	Planning
Mind reading	Listening
Whining	Valuing
Withdrawing	Validating
	Mirroring

Complete handouts are located in the appendix.

Provide Instructional Commentary. Stop the Role Play and indicate that you are stepping out of your role. (You may move to a different side of the room to indicate clearly that you are not in the Role Play.) Begin by asking participants to comment on what has happened in the Role Play so far, using the glossary or the checklist as a framework. Prompt participants to ensure that they identify all relevant concepts and procedures.

> *During the discussion, participants have no difficulty identifying Kevin's behaviors as examples of partial acceptance, excuses, and counterattacks. Some participants appear to be confused about the distinction between denial and partial acceptance. Kevin takes this opportunity to clarify the distinction between these two states of being.*

Continue to Role Play and Analyze. Check with the other volunteer to see if he or she would like to step out of the role and give someone else a turn. Continue to Role Play and portray other concepts or procedures. Stop the Role Play from time to time, step out of the role, and discuss the instructional content.

Kevin continues working through the Role Play and the instructional content. Later, he portrays some positive behaviors, such as listening and mirroring. During the discussion segments, participants identify Kevin's different positive and negative behaviors.

Change the Scenario and Players. If necessary, describe a new Role Play situation to permit the enactment of other types of behaviors. Conduct the new Role Play with different participants. Stop from time to time to insert instructional commentaries.

Kevin describes a new scenario involving an absent-minded database manager who loses a chunk of data because he forgot to save the entries. He is about to have a meeting with his supervisor. Kevin selects Carlos and Peggy to play the roles. Just before the Role Play begins, Kevin whispers to Carlos to take an apologetic, positive stance.

Conclude the Presentation. Do not attempt to present all concepts or procedures using Role Play, because it is far too time consuming. Discuss additional items, summarize key points, and invite participants to ask questions and make comments.

None of the volunteers has an opportunity to demonstrate the concepts of denial, whining, problem identification, or planning. Kevin briefly discusses each of these concepts. Participants' questions and comments suggest that they have mastered the concepts.

What If...

There Is Not Enough Time? You can do fewer, shorter Role Plays and comment only on key learning points.

There Is No Competent Role Player? Prepare a participant in advance. Provide this participant with a cue card containing appropriate lines to illustrate different concepts or procedures. Or use a videotape recording of a Role Play. If all else fails, carry out an imaginary dialog in which you play both roles.

The Role Player Gets Carried Away? If you lose control of the Role Play, stop it. Describe and explain the appropriate topics. Set up a new scenario and select a new player.

Concluding Thoughts

All five interactive lecture formats presented in this chapter require and reward participants to use flexible learning tools. Idea Maps are an effective substitute for the traditional forms of outlining and note taking. Intelligent Interruptions involve flexible responses and reactions to new information and concepts. Interactive Stories encourage collaborative analysis and problem solving. Job Aids introduce participants to a new approach for improving their performance with just-in-time instructions and information. Role Plays help participants transform abstract concepts into personal behaviors.

What would happen if we replaced these interspersed tasks with test questions? This is the approach used in the interactive lecture formats explored in the next chapter. The test questions, however, are not presented as boring or frightening devices. Instead, they become puzzle elements in a game-like setting.

Integrated Quizzes

Quiz contests provide highly motivating review activities. Instead of sandwiching different learning tasks into your lecture, you can use different types of quizzes.

Stop your presentation from time to time and conduct a quiz activity. After each quiz, discuss errors and misconceptions revealed in participants' responses. Continue your lecture, alternating between lecture and quiz sessions until you have covered the entire training content. This chapter offers four types of quizzes:

- *Bingo:* This game uses Bingo cards to encourage interaction.
- *Crossword:* This game uses a Crossword puzzle format to test the mastery of the major points from your lecture.
- *EG Hunt:* This activity uses examples to illustrate concepts presented in your lecture.
- *Team Quiz:* This game will help participants remember what was presented.

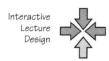

Bingo

I have always been fascinated with Bingo and its variants. This lecture game uses Bingo cards to encourage interaction.

Key Feature

The presenter gives a lecture and asks questions at random intervals. Participants pair up, examine their Bingo card, and place a check mark on the square that contains the correct answer to a given question.

When to Use This Game

Bingo works best when the instructional content is primarily factual or conceptual and when the participants are capable of working with partners. You must be able to generate several short-answer questions related to the content of the presentation.

Sample Topics

This list includes just a few areas that would lend themselves well to Bingo:

- basic computer terminology
- cultural norms in Asian countries
- introduction to symbolic logic
- investing in mutual funds
- management concepts from around the world
- new employee orientation.

Supplies

These items are both necessary and helpful during the implementation of Bingo:

- Bingo cards, each with a unique arrangement of 25 words or phrases
- A handout with list of questions.

Flow

Prepare for the Activity. Before the presentation, prepare an outline and divide it into 10- to 15-minute sections. For each section, prepare a set of short-answer questions. Assemble the questions and print them on transparencies or handouts. Make a list of the answers. Prepare Bingo cards that have these answers arranged in a five-by-five matrix. It is not necessary for every answer to appear on each card. If you have more than 25 answers, distribute them evenly among the different cards.

John's presentation is on commercial opportunities in East European countries. He decides to divide the presentation into five sections: economic climate, government regulations, status of free-market enterprise, tax laws and regulations, and marketing strategies. For each section, he generates a set of five to eight questions such as, "In which country is Microelectronica, Inc., located?" Using the answers, he prepares several different Bingo cards. Figure 4-1 shows one of the cards he created.

Brief the Participants. Before the presentation, ask participants to pair up. Give each pair a card. If you have an odd number of participants, the last person should join one of the pairs rather than work alone. Explain that you will ask questions during the lecture. Each pair should find the answer to each question on its card and place a pencil check mark in that square. At the end of the lecture, the pair with the most sets of five marked squares in a horizontal, vertical, or diagonal line is the winner. Stress the importance of paying attention to the content of the lecture during the presentation and working together with partners to find the answers.

John explains the Bingo lecture format to the participants. Because he has 17 participants, he creates a triad to share the last Bingo card.

Figure 4-1. John's Bingo card.

radioactive products and drugs	Pilsudski's coup d'etat	Bratislava Stock Exchange	Defense Minister Hain Rebas	carbonate meal
economically depressed regions	repatriation of foreign currency	free trade zones	Comecon	bank guarantees
import restrictions	value-added tax	restricted sectors	availability of skilled labor force	investment incentives
Most Favored Nation status	Czech and Slovak Federal Republic	Estonian Supreme Council	Latvian parliament	Micro-electronica
Ministry of Foreign Economic Relations	1,000,000 Slovak crowns	introduction of new technologies	Estonian Fatherland Party	*perestroika*

Start the Presentation. Make a presentation on the first section of the topic. Stop the lecture and tell participants that the first question interlude is about to begin.

John begins with a discussion about the economy of the Baltic states of Latvia, Lithuania, and Estonia. He then discusses Bulgaria's bank shake-up before announcing the first question interlude.

Present Questions for the First Section. Project the transparency with these questions or give a copy of the questions to each partnership. Ask participants to work with their partners and come up with answers. Ask them to scan their Bingo cards and place check marks on the squares that con-

tain the correct answers. Inform participants that not every card contains all answers. Pause while participants place the check marks.

John decides to distribute a handout with the questions rather than project them on the overhead screen. The pairs get excited and discuss the questions. In the process, the partners compare their notes and argue with each other. Eventually, they place check marks in the squares that contain the answers. One of the pairs claims that its card doesn't have any answers. John knows this is unlikely, but tells them that they will probably have numerous answers during the next question interlude.

Have Participants Check Their Answers. Request that each pair give its Bingo card to a nearby pair. Read each of the questions and give the correct answer. Ask the pairs to look over the Bingo cards to see if the square with the answer is marked. If it is, have them write "OK" in the square. After you have answered all the questions, ask the pairs to look over cards for any check marks in squares that do not have an "OK." If they find any such check marks, they should erase them. When the pairs are finished, have them return the cards to their owners.

Whenever a pair gets back a corrected card with five marked squares in a line horizontally, vertically, or diagonally, they should shout "Bingo!" However, they should continue playing, because the pair with the most lines of five at the end of the session is the winner.

One of the pairs complains that the check marks are so light that they are almost invisible. John asks them to give the other pair the benefit of the doubt.

Repeat the Process. Continue your lecture by presenting the next section. Repeat the process of stopping the lecture and playing the next Bingo round following the same style as in the first, supervising each round, and providing feedback for correct answers. Again, winners should continue playing.

John goes through his presentation with great enthusiasm. The participants are particularly impressed with his insightful discussion of Central Europe and the European Union's growth.

Conclude the Activity. At the end of the last round of questions, ask all of the participants to check their cards and count one point for each horizontal, vertical, or diagonal line of five marked squares. Identify the pair with the most Bingos. Congratulate the winners and, if you can afford it, give them an appropriate prize.

One of the pairs has all but one square correctly marked. They are the winners with a high score of 10 Bingos.

What If...

You Don't Have Time to Create Bingo Cards? Purchase a copy of ZINGO, which is a computer program for IBM-compatible machines. ZINGO generates and prints random Bingo cards on an HP LaserJet printer.

You Want a Cheaper Alternative? Hand out blank Bingo cards and a set of answer words or phrases before beginning the presentation. Ask participants to copy these answers onto their cards in random order. If you have more than 25 answers,

---

How to Print 65,001 Different Bingo Cards

If you want to print Bingo cards the easy and fast way, you need a copy of the ZINGO program. To use this program, all you need to do is type 25 words, phrases, short sentences, or questions on a simple template. When you click a button, ZINGO prints out up to 65,001 different arrangements of your words or phrases as Bingo cards. The latest version of the ZINGO software program includes these features:

- print preview
- spell checking
- sorting of items
- support for any printer
- support for any typeface
- easy-to-use template on the screen
- individual numbering of each card
- choice of type face, size, and style for the title, items, and card number
- cards with grids of any dimension from 2×2 to 7×7 (including rectangular grids)

This $40 software package can be ordered online at www.thiagi.com or by telephone (812.332.1478).

tell participants to leave out some of them at random. Gather up the cards; proceed as above giving a card to each pair.

There Is Not Enough Time? Play the Bingo game at the end of the entire presentation. Reserve the final five minutes for the question interlude. If you cannot even spare that amount of time, give the Bingo cards and a set of questions as a homework assignment.

The Group Is Too Large or Too Small? This format works well with groups of all sizes. If you have too many people, assemble them into teams of up to five members. If you have too few people, let each participant play individually.

You Want to Make the Game More Exciting? Leave some blank spaces on the card. Inform participants that if they do not find the correct answer to a question on the card, they can write the answer in a blank square.

You Don't Want to Prepare Handouts or Transparencies? Ask the questions orally. Make sure you pause long enough for partners to locate the correct square and place a check mark in it. Give the answer to each question and have the neighboring partners verify the answers before moving on to the next question.

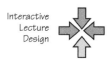

Crossword

Most people are familiar with Crossword puzzles; some even seem to be addicted to them! Very few people can resist the temptation to scan the clues and fill in at least a few answers while waiting at an airport or dentist's office. With the easy availability of Crossword software, people are using these puzzles more frequently in training situations.

Participants work in pairs to encourage mutual learning and find the answers in a Crossword puzzle related to the training topic. Stop your lecture from time to time to provide puzzle-solving interludes. Before continuing the lecture, provide feedback and clarification based on how successful the participants were in solving the puzzle based on what you explored in your preceding presentation.

Key Feature

Participants receive a Crossword puzzle handout that contains clues to test the mastery of the major learning points in the presentation. During puzzle-solving interludes, participants pair up and solve as much of the puzzle as possible.

Supplies

These items are both necessary and helpful during the implementation of a Crossword activity:

- Crossword puzzle handout, one copy for each pair of participants
- timer
- whistle.

When to Use This Format

Crossword puzzles are appropriate when the instructional content contains factual and technical information. They are particularly useful in situations where participants are unfamiliar with the training content, but recall of technical terms, acronyms, and abbreviations is a critical job requirement.

Sample Topics

This list includes just a few areas that would lend themselves well to Crosswords:

- product knowledge
- programming languages
- export policies
- quality award criteria
- conflict of interest
- plant safety.

Preparation

The Crossword lecture format does require some preparation. Before your presentation, you need to construct your puzzle. Here are the steps to ensure that your puzzles provide maximum instructional value.

Prepare an Outline. List the topics and subtopics that you plan to cover.

Raja will be conducting an introductory session about the Internet. He begins with an outline that contains these six topics:

I. *Modems*
II. *The Internet*
III. *Email*
IV. *Web browsers*
V. *Chat rooms*
VI. *Advanced topics.*

Here are the subtopics for the topic of email that he plans to cover during his lecture:

A. *Bright side*

1. *Increasing use of email*
2. *Advantages of email (speed and low cost)*
3. *Email attachments.*

B. *Dark side*

    1. *Junk email*

    2. *Flaming*

    3. *Viruses and worms.*

Convert the Outline Into a Series of Questions. Work from the lowest level of your outline. Come up with two or three short-answer questions related to key content elements.

Prepare a List of Answers. List all answers to questions generated in the previous step. Make sure that each answer is a single word. If necessary, rewrite the question.

Raja started out by coming up with a few short-answer questions and their answers:

- *What label identifies junk email? (spam)*
- *What dangerous things can email messages transmit? (viruses)*
- *What is an angry exchange of email messages called? (flame)*
- *What is the special name for a document enclosed with an email message? (attachment)*

Create the Crossword Puzzle. Convert your questions into Crossword puzzle clues. You can use computer software to construct the Crossword grid.

Modify the Puzzle. You may not be able to create a puzzle that uses all the questions on your list. Examine the puzzle to ensure a balanced distribution of questions from different units in the outline. If necessary, add more items to the puzzle.

Figure 4-2 shows what Raja's puzzle looks like. You have the clues and the blank grid in case you want to solve the puzzle and check your own Internet IQ.

Flow

Introduce the Topic. At the beginning of your training session, announce your objec-tives and briefly explain the format. Tell par-ticipants that you will interrupt your lecture presentation from time to time so they can work with a partner to solve a Crossword puzzle. Emphasize the importance of paying close attention to your lecture so that they can solve the puzzle successfully. Ask partic-ipants to pair up.

During the training session, Raja asks participants to choose a partner and explains the interactive lecture format.

Distribute Copies of the Puzzle. Give a copy of the Crossword puzzle (clues and the numbered blank grid) to each pair.

Raja gives one copy of the Crossword puzzle to each participant even though participants will all be working in pairs.

Pretest the Group. Ask participants to take a couple of minutes working in pairs to solve as much of the Crossword puzzle as possible. This step serves three important purposes:

- It familiarizes participants with the clues and provides a preview of the training content.
- It establishes a baseline so partici-pants can realize how much they have learned at the end of the session.
- It gives you a feel for the entry level of the participants (what they already know about your training topic) so you can adjust your pres-entation to suit their needs.

Raja invites participants to work with their partners to solve the puzzle. As he expected, most people were able to write down only one or two items.

Make Your Presentation. Deliver a lecture related to the first unit in your outline. Be sure to explore all relevant topics, includ-ing those that are not required to solve the puzzle. Be sure to provide information

Figure 4-2. The Crossword puzzle Raja distributed for his lecture.

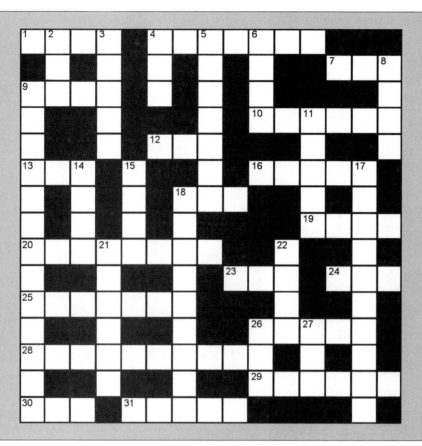

CLUES

Across

1. Unsolicited email
4. Place on the Internet with a home page and other pages (sometimes two words)
7. Preferred term for measuring modem speed (abbr.)
9. An old-fashioned measurement unit for modem speed
10. Tool that allows a user to move around a Website (abbr.)
12. Popular in late '80s as a place to chat and to transfer files (abbr.)
13. Local Exchange Carrier (abbr.)
16. Ancient Romans and modern surfers use this word for a discussion group
18. Location of a resource on the Web or the address of a Webpage (abbr.)
19. One of the things you can do on eBay
20. Small version of Internet used within a Local Area Network
23. Short for Internet
24. Short for binary digit
25. Type of logic used in Internet searches
26. Angry email message that can start a "war"
28. File included with an email message
29. Small program that adds a specific feature to a larger program (two words)
30. Shorter name for a period
31. Downloading a program can be easier than installing from these

Down

2. Hand-held device that you can use to connect to the Web (abbr.)
3. Device that permits your computer to communicate over a phone line
4. You need 5 Down to view this (abbr.)
5. Software used to navigate the Web
6. Small graphic that represents a file or a program
8. To explore the Web without a specific goal
9. Post your messages here (two words)
11. Email can sometimes carry a malicious _____
14. Having a conversation over the Internet by typing messages
15. Sun Microsystems' programming language for the Web
17. Combination of text, sound, photo, and video
18. Nicknames or handles that people use on the Web
21. To clean out an old cached version you may have to refresh or do this
22. A language used to create Webpages (abbr.)
26. A standard method for transferring files over the Internet (abbr.)
27. Address-generating unit (abbr.)

necessary to solve all Crossword puzzle items related to this unit.

Raja begins with an explanation of different types of modems.

Announce a Puzzle-Solving Interlude. Stop your lecture presentation and ask partners to work with each other to solve as much of the puzzle as possible. Set a suitable time limit.

Raja stops his presentation after five minutes and invites participants to continue solving the puzzle. Don and Rick, working as partners, immediately fill out the words for 7 across and 9 across. They continue reviewing other clues.

Give Feedback. Stop the puzzle-solving activity when the time expires. Identify appropriate clues and give the answers. Ask participants to raise their hands if they had the right answers. If there are only a few hands raised, provide some clarification and explanation. If some participants claim to have solved additional items, congratulate them and ask them to hold the answer until the next round.

Most participants indicate that they have solved 3 down, 7 across, 9 across, and 24 across. Raja confirms the correct answers. Don reports that he has solved three more clues. Raja thanks them for sharing their progress.

Continue Your Lecture. Present the content related to the next unit in your outline. As before, stop the lecture to conduct another round of puzzle solving and provide feedback. Repeat this procedure as often as needed.

Raja continues his lecture and provides five more puzzle-solving interludes.

Crossword Compiler

I have evaluated more than 20 software programs for creating Crossword puzzles. Without a doubt, the best one is Antony Lewis's Crossword Compiler program. I use this program almost every day to create Crossword puzzles for my training workshops and for export to my Website. If you are planning to create and use Crossword puzzles for instructional purposes, I strongly recommend that you invest $49 in this software program.

Here are some exciting things that you can do with Crossword Compiler:

1. *Create instructional puzzles.* Type in technical terms and key words associated with your training content. Ask Crossword Compiler to build a Crossword puzzle using these words. The computer incorporates as many of your words as possible. Edit the puzzle and add additional words. Then type your clues in the form of test questions.
2. *Print your puzzle.* Copy the puzzle to the clipboard or save it as a file. Selectively export the puzzle, solution, numbered solution, clues, answers, and explanations. I export my puzzles in Rich Text Format and print it—grid and all—using Microsoft Word. You can also export the puzzle as bitmap, GIF, TIFF, or metafile.
3. *Display your puzzle on your Website.* This is my favorite part of Crossword Compiler. Export your Crossword puzzle as an interactive puzzle that you or someone else can solve on screen. The program includes license to use this interactive applet on one Website. To experience the ease of solving a puzzle on the Web, visit http://www.thiagi.com/cp-elearning.html.
4. *Learn by using the electronic performance support system.* The program has an extensive context-sensitive help function. If you get stuck, just press a button to get a detailed job aid related to what you are trying to do.

Visit the Crossword Compiler Website at http://www.Crossword-compiler.com/cgi-bin/cooklink.pl?thiagi to download a demo or order it online. (Disclosure: The Thiagi Group receives a small payment if you use this link to purchase the product.)

Conclude the Session. At the end of the last puzzle-solving interlude, give the solution sheet to all participants. Ask them to verify their answers. Invite participants to ask questions about anything that is unclear. Provide brief answers.

Figure 4-3. The solution to Raja's Crossword puzzle.

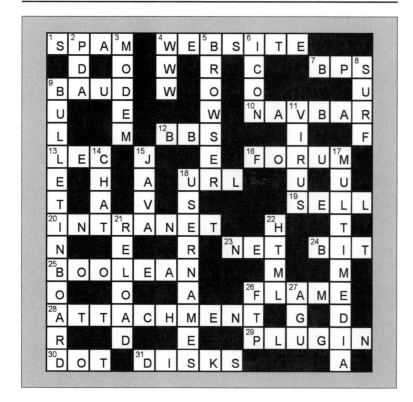

After the last puzzle-solving interlude, Raja gives everyone the official solution sheet (figure 4-3).

What If...

There Is Not Enough Time? Use the Crossword puzzle at the end of your presentation as the final test. Give participants five minutes to solve the entire puzzle, working in pairs or teams. Give them the solution sheet for a self-check. You can even distribute the Crossword puzzle at the end of your presentation as a follow-up activity for participants to solve at their leisure.

You Cannot Incorporate All the Questions in the Crossword Puzzle? Print the list of additional questions and distribute them at the end of the session. Ask participants to review the list and identify any questions that they cannot answer. Provide short answers and explanations.

You Don't Know How to Design a Crossword Puzzle? Let your computer do it! There are many computer programs available to help you with this task.

EG Hunt

The most effective way to teach a concept is to illustrate it with examples. The most valid way to test the mastery of a concept is to ask the learner to generate examples. EG Hunt (in which "e.g." refers to examples) uses this testing strategy as its core element.

Key Feature

The presenter defines and discusses different concepts, stops the lecture from time to time, and asks the participants to generate or select specific examples of a concept.

When to Use This Game

EG Hunt is most effectively used if the instructional content contains several concepts that you have analyzed in terms of critical and variable features. It is also necessary that your participants be capable of generating appropriate examples.

Sample Topics

This list includes just a few areas that would lend themselves well to EG Hunt:

- architectural styles
- ways to conclude a lecture
- domains of learning
- management styles
- personality types
- types of humor.

Preparation

To implement EG Hunt, you will have to prepare a handout listing concepts and their definitions, and you should assemble a portfolio of examples if the participants are going to be required to recognize, rather than generate, examples.

Flow

Begin With a Preview. Present the big picture, showing the framework and the relationship among the concepts.

Pietro's presentation is on the principles of performance technology. In his preview, he talks about different causes for performance problems. He explains that these causes can be divided into internal and external types and subdivided into skill and knowledge deficits, motivational deficits, and environmental deficits. Each of these deficits, in turn, can be further divided into other specific types.

Define Each Concept. Identify its critical and irrelevant features. Illustrate the concept with several examples.

Pietro defines skill and knowledge deficits as not knowing what, when, or how to do different things. As an infallible method for identifying this type of performance problem, he suggests the $1 million test: If a person cannot perform a task even if offered a huge sum of money, it is a case of skill and knowledge deficit. For example, Pietro explains that he could not write a sonnet in Portuguese on the spot, even if someone offered him a huge sum of money.

Organize Participants Into Teams. Ideally, you should have three to five teams, each with three to seven members. Ask the teams to come up with a specific example. Set up competition among teams if that would result in an appropriate level of motivation.

Participants quickly organize into four teams of six members. Team members turn their chairs around and brainstorm a clear example of skill and knowledge deficit. David is the only man on a team with five women. After

Delivering a lecture is a bit like prospecting for black gold. If you don't strike oil in 10 minutes, stop boring.

some discussion, they decide that insensitive behaviors on the part of most male managers are due to a lack of knowledge about what values are important to women. David does not feel this is a clear example, but he keeps his mouth shut for fear of being insensitive.

Ask Teams to Present Their Examples. Select the teams in a random order. Explain that it is very important for the other teams to pay attention. Listen carefully to each example; ask the team for clarification if necessary.

Monica, a member of David's team, acts as its spokesperson and reports on the example of an insensitive male manager. Examples from the other teams include a child choking to death because nobody knows the Heimlich maneuver, and a company that incurs a heavy fine because somebody did not know that lithium peroxide should not be over-packed with acetone.

Have Participants Rate Examples. Point to each team and ask members of the other teams to raise their hands if they believe that this team came up with the best example of a specific type. Make sure that participants rate every team in this peer-polling process. Skip this step if you do not want to stress the element of competition.

Pietro takes a few minutes to conduct a poll. The most popular example turns out to be the child choking to death because nobody knows the Heimlich maneuver.

Comment on the Examples. Give appropriate feedback on each example, highlighting the critical and variable features. Correct any misconceptions and clarify definitions.

Pietro says that the Heimlich maneuver example is a clear performance problem that is obviously due to a skill deficit. He emphasizes that even if people know what to do in a choking situation, without the skill to remedy the situation they still suffer from a skill and knowledge deficit. He makes similar comments on the other examples.

Continue With the Presentation. Define and explain other concepts. Intersperse the presentation with team sessions that require generating new examples according to your specifications.

Pietro continues by talking about motivational deficits and its subcategories. Among the examples generated by the teams is an imaginary manager's statement: "If you finish the project ahead of time, we'll transfer you to Rawlins, Wyoming!"

Review the Concepts. Near the conclusion of the session, ask for a series of related examples.

After reviewing all the categories of performance-problem causes, Pietro asks the teams to come up with a series of related examples. David's team comes up with the best collection: "Anybody can read a page written at the sixth-grade level, but if we give you a sixth-grade Swahili textbook, you will suffer from a skill and knowledge deficit. If we use a sixth-grade English book but turn the lights off in a dark room, you will suffer from an environmental deficit. If we ask you to read aloud from a collection of dirty jokes, you will probably (and fortunately) suffer from a motivational deficit."

What If...

There Is Not Enough Time? Reduce the number of team sessions. Define and explain several concepts, but ask the teams to come up with an example of just one.

There Are Too Many Teams? Ask all teams to generate examples, but have only two teams present theirs. Ask the other teams to decide which example best meets your specifications.

Teams Are Tired of the Same Task? Use a variety of categories: easy to recognize, subtle, humorous, imaginative, futuristic, inexpensive, graphic, politically correct, and childish. Emphasize that the example should have all the critical features of the concept but may vary in its other features to meet your specifications.

The Teams Cannot Generate Examples? If you are teaching about styles of medieval architecture, it will be impractical for the teams to generate a Gothic cathedral. You can, however, ask them to draw a picture of an imaginary cathedral or write a descriptive paragraph for an imaginary encyclopedia of architectural styles.

The Topic Is Too Technical? If participants are unlikely to generate examples because of the complexity of the task or time limitations, give the teams a handout with a wide variety of examples. Ask the teams to select the examples of a specific type from this portfolio. Reward the teams for their speed and thoroughness.

You Want the Teams to Talk About Their Examples? If you are using a handout with a wide variety of examples, you can ask the teams to select the single best example of a specific type. During the reporting period, each team identifies its example and gives a brief justification for its choice. The team that provides the most convincing justification wins.

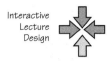

Team Quiz

To give a dramatic demonstration of lecture games, I usually begin by asking for a volunteer who is an enthusiastic expert on some esoteric topic. I ask this person to make a three-minute presentation to the group, loading as many facts into this lecture as possible. Then I use the Team Quiz format to show how effectively lecture games work.

Key Feature

During a data-dump presentation, if participants do not use it, they lose it. This game prevents rapid decay of new information by forcing participants to use it at frequent intervals. Quiz sessions during which participants come up with questions and answers break up the lecture presentation.

When to Use This Format

Team Quiz works best when the instructional content involves significant amounts of technical information or conceptual topics. Of course, your participants should be capable of working in teams and asking valid questions, and you must have technical expertise and at least a rough outline for the presentation.

Sample Topics

This list includes just a few areas that would lend themselves well to Team Quiz:

- basic principles of quantum physics
- compiler construction
- introduction to the OS/2 operating system
- ISO 9000 standards
- ray tracing and radiosity
- using quality award criteria for internal assessment.

Supplies

These items are both necessary and helpful during the implementation of Team Quiz:

- timer
- whistle
- paper and pencil.

Flow

Brief Participants. Explain that your presentation will be interspersed with short quiz contests in which teams will ask questions of each other. Emphasize that it is very important to listen carefully and to take good notes. Do not distribute handouts until the end of the session. The idea is to force participants to listen carefully and take notes. Set a timer for approximately 10 minutes and explain that the first Team Quiz will begin when the timer goes off.

Madeleine is giving a presentation on distribution channels. In a brief preview, she explains that her topic deals with the ways that merchandise travels from the manufacturer to the customer. She warns participants about the Team Quiz.

Deliver the First Presentation Segment. Deliver the lecture in your normal style. Stop the presentation, in the middle of a sentence if necessary, when the timer goes off.

Madeleine talks about the vendors on one side and the end users on the other. She identifies direct sales and indirect sales as the two major categories of distribution activity. She then identifies and discusses such channels as mail order, direct marketing, industrial distributors, national wholesalers, and retail chains. She gives examples of each distribution channel and comments on its advantages and disadvantages. The timer cuts her off while she is rattling off the names of major retail chains.

Ask Teams to Develop Questions. Instruct participants to form teams of three to seven members. Make sure that you have at least three and not more than five teams. Ask the team members to compare notes, discuss what they heard during this segment of the lecture, and come up with a set of questions. At least one of these questions should be of the fact-recall, rote-memory type, for which there is a definite correct answer. Give an example of this type of question from the content you presented.

At least one of the other questions should be of the open-ended, divergent-thinking variety. This question may require evaluation, synthesis, or inferential thinking. Although it should be based on the content of the presentation, the answer should go beyond the participant merely recalling what you said. Give an example of this kind of question. Emphasize that these questions are for the participants themselves and not for you. Finally, tell the teams that they have three minutes for the question-construction activity.

Madeleine's audience consists of 21 people. They organize themselves into three teams of five members and one team of six. Madeleine gives her instructions and uses several questions as examples. For the rote-memory variety, she asks, "What are the two major types of distribution activity?" For the open-ended variety, she asks, "Which type of distribution channel do you think will be predominant by the year 2010?"

Teams get busy discussing possible questions. One of the teams asks Madeleine for clarification, but she smiles and says, "I am not available for consultation." As Madeleine walks around and listens, she is sometimes elated and sometimes depressed by what participants have gotten from her presentation.

Ask Fact-Recall Questions. At the end of three minutes, ask the teams to stop their question-construction activity. Announce that you will conduct the first phase of the quiz contest. Explain that this phase will be a closed-book activity, and ask everyone to close their notebooks and avoid talking to each other. Select one team at random and ask its spokesperson to read the fact-recall question. The questioning team selects an individual from any other team. If this person gives a correct answer, his or her team gets 2 points. If this person consults with the team and gives the correct answer, the team gets 1 point. If the person gives an incorrect answer, the team loses a point. If the person gives an incorrect answer after consultation, the team loses 2 points. Ask the questioning team to select an individual. After hearing the answer, allow the team to decide if it is correct or not.

Madeleine explains the procedure and suggests that the teams need not worry about keeping track of the scores because she will do that. The first team asks its question: "What is the name of a major national distributor?" and picks on Mark, who seems to be avoiding eye contact with the questioner. Much to everyone's surprise, Mark immediately gives the correct answer. His team applauds his effort. Other teams take turns asking their fact-recall questions. Only one participant has to consult with her team members before giving the correct answer.

Ask Open-Ended Questions. After all teams have had an opportunity to ask a fact-recall question, announce that you are moving on to open-ended questions. During this phase, team members can refer to their notes and talk to each other. One team asks its question and pauses for 30 seconds while the other teams prepare their answers. Then the questioning team selects a team. Its spokesperson gives the team's answer. Any other team that thinks it can provide a superior answer can challenge this answer. If there is no challenge, the answering team receives 3 points. If there is a challenge, then the questioning team listens to the alternative answer and decides which team did a better job. The winner receives 3 points.

Madeleine selects Claire to ask her team's open-ended question. Claire asks, "How would you classify the shopping channels on cable TV, and why do you think that your classification is correct?" Someone hums the "Jeopardy" tune in the background as different teams prepare their responses. Ivan acts as the spokesperson for the selected team. He gives the classification as direct sales and provides a lengthy justification. When he pauses, Don's team challenges this response. After listening to the new response, Claire's team decides that the original answer was actually the better one. Members of Ivan's team applaud themselves for earning 3 points.

Continue With Your Presentation. Begin by commenting on the participants' questions and answers, and remedy any misconceptions revealed during the Team Quiz. Then continue with your presentation, warning participants that the next quiz session will be in about 10 minutes.

Madeleine uses the open-ended question about the shopping channels as a springboard for the continuation of her lecture. She talks about the distribution trends.

Repeat the Process and Conclude the Session. When the timer goes off, ask participants to work in their teams as before and to prepare the same types of questions covering the new topics you presented. After three minutes, conduct the quiz contest. Continue with more segments of your presentation until you have covered all the important topics.

Madeleine repeats the procedure twice before she completes her lecture. After her final presentation, she tells participants that they will skip the last quiz session. She thanks them for the quality of their questions and answers.

What If...

There Is Not Enough Time? Schedule the quiz sessions once every 20 minutes instead of every 10 minutes. Instruct every team to come up with its questions, but direct only a couple of teams to ask questions.

The Questions Are Not Effective? Give some feedback on the quality of the questions. Before the lecture, train participants to come up with good questions. Give them a checklist on how to ask different kinds of questions by using appropriate examples. As a variation during a Team Quiz session, ask all teams to read their questions. Instead of giving answers, ask each team to decide which team, excluding itself, came up with the best set of questions. Award points to this team.

There Are Too Many Participants? You will not have time for all teams to ask questions, so just ask a couple of teams for their questions.

The Answers Reveal Major Misunderstandings? This is actually an advantage. Before launching into the next segment of your presentation, take a few minutes to correct these misunderstandings.

A Team Accepts an Incorrect Answer or Rejects a Correct One? Do not correct the error during the quiz. Wait for the next segment of your presentation, clarify the situation, and provide appropriate explanations. Correct the team's score.

You Are Not a Subject Matter Expert? Invite one or more experts to make the presentation while you act as a game-show host.

Concluding Thoughts

Here are some notes from the field about this type of interactive lectures:

- I have used Team Quiz in 25 different countries. It works effectively with trainers and participants in different cultures with varying traditional approaches to education and training. Crossword puzzles also work around the world. Participants in different countries and cultures enjoy solving these puzzles in their own languages.
- EG Hunt requires participants to apply abstract definitions to specific examples in different topics ranging from hard-skill areas such as programming syntax to such soft-skill areas as empathy.
- Participants' interest level in the Bingo format remains high throughout the activity because it combines chance element with the mastery of the training comment.

In the type of interactive lecture format explored in this chapter, participants are presented with the quiz after they listen to a segment of the lecture. What would happen if you turned this sequence around and presented the quiz before the lecture? In the next chapter, I introduce four different formats in which the quiz is used as a pretest, and the lecture is based on participants' performance on this test.

Assessment-Based Learning

In assessment-based learning interactive lectures, participant involvement advances to the beginning of the training session. You administer an appropriate test at the beginning of the session. Using the information revealed by participants' responses, you select units of your lecture content and arrange them in a suitable sequence to efficiently close the gaps in their knowledge. The exercises in this chapter are as follows:

- *Confusion:* This card-swapping game allows participants to share their confusion about a lecture without embarrassment.

- *FAQs and Fakes:* Here's a game that tests participants' understanding and recall of lecture content using a format much like the "frequently asked questions" section of a Website.

- *Questionnaire Analysis:* This technique uses a self-scoring questionnaire to explore important topics in your lecture.

- *Shouting Match:* This method can be used to explore controversial topics such as misconceptions and prejudices.

Interactive
Lecture
Format

Confusion

Even the clearest presentation is likely to confuse at least a few audience members. Setting aside ample time to answer questions from the audience is an effective strategy to clarify your ideas. This interactive lecture uses a card-swapping strategy to help participants share any confusion they might have while eschewing the embarrassment that often comes from revealing a personal knowledge gap.

Key Feature

Participants anonymously ask questions about confusing and difficult aspects of your presentation. Answer these questions and use a simple strategy to help participants recall and summarize key concepts.

When to Use This Format

The Confusion activity has been most advantageous under the following circumstances:

- the instructional content includes more concepts and principles than facts
- participants have different amounts of previous knowledge
- key concepts can be clearly identified.

Sample Topics

The following topics are just a few examples of the types of information that Confusion can be effectively used for:

- basic accounting principles
- behavioral interviewing
- career planning
- project management
- means of selling professional services.

Supplies

To use Confusion successfully, you need the following two items:

- index cards on which the participants may write their questions
- a whistle.

Flow

Explain the Format. Tell participants that you are going to set aside half of the allotted lecture time to respond to questions from the audience. Warn participants that your initial presentation will be fairly fast-paced and encourage them to take useful notes.

Sayid is making a presentation on U.S. corporate benefits to a group of 15 customer service associates at a help-desk facility in Manila. He has 50 minutes for his presentation and explains that he is planning to spend half of that time for the question-and-answer session.

Make Your Presentation. Present the information in a logical and coherent fashion. Do not provide unnecessary and redundant explanations. Because an abundance of time is being reserved for questions later on, discourage questions from the audience at this stage. Conclude your presentation quickly so as not to intrude on the question-and-answer time.

Sayid spends five minutes on each of these four topics:

- *health and welfare plans*
- *defined contributions*
- *defined benefits*
- *trends in U.S. corporations.*

He takes care not to rush through the content too quickly. Instead, he focuses on presenting a few key concepts related to each topic.

Ask Participants to Write Questions. Invite them to review their notes, think about what they heard, and recall difficult, incomplete, or confusing topics about which they would like to have additional information. Distribute two blank index cards to each participant. Ask them to write a question that they would like to have answered on each card. Tell participants to work independently and set a one-minute time limit for this part of the activity.

Shannon immediately writes this question on one of the cards: "What exactly do you mean by the portability of the defined-benefit plan? I do not understand how a corporation will let an employee take his pension funds to a new employer." After reviewing her notes, she comes up with a question for the second card: "Can an employee transfer funds from a defined-contribution plan to a defined-benefit plan?"

Redistribute Question Cards. At the end of the minute, blow a whistle and ask participants to complete their two questions. Instruct all participants to hold their question cards with the written side down, stand up, move around, and keep exchanging cards with each other without reading the questions around for about 30 seconds. Ask participants to return to their seats with the two cards they most recently received.

The questions that Shannon ends up with at the end of the card exchange are: "Can we classify Social Security

as a defined benefit?" and "What does the word 'vested' mean?"

Explain the Procedure. Point out that participants do not know whose questions they currently have so no one needs to worry about appearing foolish by asking silly questions. Invite participants to take turns reading questions. Or, if you feel like adding a playful alternative to the procedure, you can invite participants to pretend to read the question from the card but actually ask a question that he or she wants answered. Encourage the participants to listen to the answers you give even if they are not to their own questions. Invite them to take notes about your answers. Warn them that a future activity requires careful note-taking and recall.

Shannon does not think that either of the questions she has is important so she decides to ask her original question if she is invited to do so. She also gets her notebook out to jot down anything she identifies as important.

Conduct the Question-and-Answer Session. Invite the first volunteer to read one of the two questions he or she has. Give a short and relevant answer. Repeat the process with additional volunteers. Encourage participants to read the most important questions because time is limited.

Sayid listens to the questions carefully and gives simple and straightforward answers.

Conclude the Question-and-Answer Session. After about 25 minutes, announce the end of the question-and-answer session. Explain that you are going to tie up some loose ends, and then make a brief presentation

Technical Glossary

Sleep walking:
   Somnambulism
Sleep talking:
   Lecture

covering important topics not explored in your earlier answers.

During the question-and-answer period, the fact that nobody asked any questions about trends in U.S. corporate benefits surprised Sayid. Therefore, he spent some time recapping important trends and predicting their future impact.

Invite Participants to Reflect on Your Presentation. Distribute additional blank index cards. Ask each participant to review his or her notes, reflect on your answers, and write down a summary sentence that captures one important idea on the index card. After a suitable pause, collect the cards with summary sentences. Randomly select three and read the sentences.

Conclude the Session. Be sure to thank the group for taking responsibility for their own learning. Acknowledge that you probably did not answer critical questions from all participants. Ask participants to collect cards with unanswered questions and give them to you. Tell participants that you will post the answers on your Website if you have such a resource at your disposal.

After removing duplicates, Sayid ends up with 17 questions. With the help of a couple of friends, he writes clear answers in plain English and posts them at the company's Website.

What If...

There Is Not Enough Time? Set aside half of whatever time you have. Remember that it is more important to clarify participants' confusion than to unload more details during your presentation.

There Are Too Many People? Ask participants to look at their questions and decide if they are important. Respond to the first five or six questions in the lecture session and respond to the rest through a frequently asked questions (FAQ) page on your own or your client's Website.

Participants Feel Left Out Because Their Questions Were Not Discussed? Collect all of the cards and tape them to the wall. Invite participants to take a "gallery walk," read the cards, and compare them with each other.

FAQs and Fakes

FAQs and Fakes

The usual training sequence is to make a presentation and then test the participants understanding and recall of the content. In FAQs and Fakes, we turn this sequence upside down by testing participants first and then presenting the relevant content.

If you have ever played the "Dictionary" game, also known as "Fictionary," you already know how to use this interactive lecture strategy. In "Dictionary," one player selects an esoteric word from a dictionary. Other players come up with and write down imaginary definitions. The person who selected the original word copies the official definition from the dictionary, collects all definitions, and reads them in random order. Other players try to guess which definition is correct. Players score points for identifying the correct definition or for writing a fake definition that fooled others.

Key Feature

Prepare a list of FAQs about the training topic. Ask the first question and invite teams to prepare fake answers. Read the answers, along with the correct answer, which you wrote, in a random order. Have the teams guess which answer is correct. Identify the correct answer and follow up with a mini-lecture related to the original question.

When to Use This Format

FAQs and Fakes is often efficacious under the following circumstances:

- You can organize instructional content into a series of equal-sized conceptual topics.
- Participants are at different entry levels.

Sample Topics

Topics for which FAQs and Fakes would be a good learning method include anything along the lines of:

- outsourcing call centers to Asian countries
- types of cultural values
- stages in the grieving process
- alternative advertising strategies
- interventions that improve human performance
- characteristics of the digital generation.

Supplies

If you're going to use this learning method, you will need:

- index cards (or paper)
- timer
- whistle.

Preparation

Prepare an Outline of Your Presentation. Select five to seven topics and identify each by a technical term or a key phrase. Arrange topics in an appropriate sequence.

Charlie is briefing some U.S. business-people before they leave on their first trip to Australia. His main training objective is to introduce the participants to Australian national traits, icons, and passions. His list of topics includes Australian cultural values, food, sports, and natural events.

Organize Participants Into Teams. Begin your session by dividing the group into three to five teams of approximately equal size. Explain that team members will collaborate in the learning process.

Charlie's audience consists of 16 business people. He divides them into two teams of five and one team of six.

Flow

Brief the Participants. Specify the overall training goal. Briefly explain the procedure to the learners. Outline how you will pose a FAQ about the training content, and teams will come up with a fake answer by using their imaginations and imitating your style. After they have their answer, the teams will present the answers created by different teams along with your official answer. Teams will then select the answer that they think is correct. Next present a mini-lecture on the topic related to the question. Teams will redefine the key phrase, and this will be repeated with other key phrases until all relevant topics are covered.

Charlie takes a slightly different approach: He explains that he will ask a sample question from one of the four topics related to Australia. He will invite teams to write the correct answer if one or more members of the team know it. Otherwise, they should write a fake answer.

The First Question. Explain that the team that has the answer most frequently chosen by other teams will earn the most points. Announce a sufficient time limit. While teams are writing their answers, write your own official answer. At the end of the time limit, collect the answers and mix them with yours.

Charlie starts with the question: What do Australians mean by the expression "tall poppy syndrome?" None of the participants have a clue, but that does not stop them from guessing wildly and coming up with fake answers. Charlie writes his own answer and collects the answers from the teams at the end of the allotted three minutes.

Time to Guess. Read all of the answers and instruct teams to vote for the answer they believe is the correct one. Be sure to keep your vocal tone even, so as not to clue participants to the correct answer. Ask teams to spend a minute collaboratively selecting the answer that they think is yours. Award 1 point to each team that selected your answer. Award 1 point to a team each time someone selects its answer.

The following list includes the correct answer written by Charlie. Can you spot it before you continue reading?

- *being proud of Australia's colorful cultural heritage*
- *cutting powerful and pretentious people down to size*
- *distilling wine from wildflower*
- *trying to outperform others in sports and leisure-time activities.*

Team C chooses the correct answer. Teams A and B choose the fake answers written by Team C. Therefore, Team C gets 3 points—1 for choosing the correct answer and 2 for fooling the other two teams. (By the way, the correct answer is cutting powerful and pretentious people down to size.)

Present Content Covered in the First Question. Move into your mini-lecture immediately after awarding scores. Use the information from the answers and the incorrect selections to diagnose participants' misconceptions.

Charlie suggests that two teams selected an incorrect answer because they were probably projecting the competitive U.S. business values. He identifies the correct answer and explains that Aussies have a tendency to be skeptical about celebrities, politicians, and entrepreneurs. He traces the origin of this national trait to the convict era and warns audience members to avoid ostentatious displays while in Australia.

Repeat the Procedure. Present the next FAQ and ask teams to create new fake answers. Collect these answers, mix them with your correct answer, and invite teams to identify the correct answer. Repeat the rest of the activities. Use the same procedure with all FAQs to cover the entire content.

> *Charlie continues his mini-lecture by identifying three other cultural traits among Australians:*
>
> - *Australian food: What is the most popular fast food in Australia?*
> - *Australian sports: Who is Sir Donald Bradman?*
> - *Natural events: What is a benefit of bushfires that occur every year in Australia?*
>
> *Meat pie is the most popular fast food in Australia, Sir Donald Bradman ("The Don") was a celebrated cricketer, and bushfires regularly clear away the undergrowth.*

What If...

There Is Not Enough Time? Use fewer questions.

There Are Too Many Participants? Do not spend time organizing them into teams. Instead, ask each participant to work on his or her own. Collect all answers and randomly select four or five. Mix up these answers with your correct answers. Read all answers and ask participants to select the correct one.

There Are Too Few Participants? Do not organize the learners into teams. Ask each participant to work alone, writing a plausible definition.

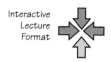

Questionnaire Analysis

Psychological instruments and question-naires intrigue people, and make them eager to discover their personal strengths and weaknesses. They are also curious about how they compare with other people. The Questionnaire Analysis format uses self-scoring questionnaires to explore important topics.

Key Feature

Participants answer a questionnaire and compute their scores. You help them interpret their scores, learn about themselves, and about the topic.

When to Use This Format

Ideal circumstances for the use of Questionnaire Analysis include, but certainly are not limited to, when:

- The instructional content involves values, attitudes, or preferences that participants can explore through a questionnaire.
- Participants are curious and competent enough to respond to a questionnaire and to score their own responses.
- You are familiar with how to use and interpret questionnaires.

Sample Topics

Topics for which Questionnaire Analysis would be appropriate include the following, along with numerous others:

- career planning
- decision-making styles
- leadership styles
- organizational climate
- personality characteristics
- gender-role stereotyping.

Handouts

You will need both a questionnaire and a scoring key to complete this activity in your interactive lecture. In addition, you may want an interpretation guideline sheet so participants can figure out what their scores mean at the end of the activity.

Flow

Introduce the Topic. Provide a brief overview of the content. Identify important topics and relate them to the questionnaire. Distribute copies of the questionnaire and briefly explain its organization.

Bill's session is about multiple forms of intelligence. He introduces the topic with examples of geniuses who scored low on traditional IQ tests and explains seven different types of intelligence—linguistic, logical, visual, musical, kinesthetic, interpersonal, and intrapersonal. He then distributes the questionnaire and walks learners through examples of the different forms of intelligence.

Explain the Format. Explain to the learners that each participant will independently complete the questionnaire and score his or her own responses. Afterward, you will help them interpret their scores and response patterns. Finally, explain how participants can use their increased self-awareness in their personal and professional lives. Explain that participants' responses will be confidential, although they can share if they want to. In potentially controversial situations (as in surveying participants for complaints against their managers), discourage participants from even voluntarily sharing their responses.

Bill explains how the format will work. Participants ask a couple of questions. They don't seem to be overly concerned about the confidentiality disclaimer because the topic does not appear to be potentially embarrassing.

Ask for Predictions. Ask that each participant estimate his or her score on the questionnaire. They should write their predictions on a piece of paper and keep it someplace safe for future reference.

Bill asks the participants to make predictions about their strongest and weakest types of intelligence. Participants take a couple of minutes to complete this activity.

Have Participants Complete the Questionnaire. Briefly review any important instructions and suggest a time limit.

Bill refers to the instructions for the questionnaire and asks the participants to review it. After a minute or so, he checks to make sure that everyone understands these instructions. He asks the participants to respond to the 56 items in the questionnaire and suggests that they should not spend more than 15 minutes doing so. Bill circulates the room during the questionnaire to assist those who need help.

Facilitate the Scoring. When all participants have finished, distribute the scoring key or explain the scoring procedure. Ask participants to score their own questionnaires, and suggest an appropriate time limit.

John distributes a two-ply carbonless scoring sheet that produces a duplicate copy. He explains that the first eight items in the questionnaire deal with linguistic intelligence, the next eight items with logical intelligence, and so on. He asks each participant to count

the number of items checked in each set and to record it as the score for that intelligence. Finally, he asks the participants to keep the original copy of the score sheet and to drop the duplicate in a box in front of the room.

Interpret the Scores. Distribute copies of the interpretation handout and walk participants through different response patterns or profiles.

Bill explains that a score of 8 indicates a strong preference for that form of intelligence, and a score of 0 identifies a form that is seldom used. Bill also talks about people with a preference for a single type of intelligence and others with a preference for two or three types. One of the participants asks which kind of preference is better. Bill explains that there is no such thing as better or worse distribution of preferences.

Provide Comparative Data. Quickly analyze the duplicate score sheets (or ask a co-facilitator to analyze them while you are busy with the previous activity). Make a summary report on your data analysis. Compare the local patterns with national norms, if the information is available.

John uses the flipchart to report the distribution of the number of participants showing the highest preference for different types of intelligences. He points out a strong bias toward linguistic intelligence and explains that teachers and trainers tend to exhibit this bias. He then gives information on the distribution of the different types among the general population.

Compare With Participants' Predictions. Ask participants to compare their actual scores with their earlier predictions. If there is a major difference, participants should try to figure out the reason.

Explain What the Scores Mean.
Suggest how they can benefit from their new awareness and invite questions to clarify different concepts.

> *Bill differentiates between linguistic and logical intelligence and between interpersonal and intrapersonal intelligence. He stresses the importance of accepting one's unique blend of intelligence and talks about the match between job requirements and types of intelligence.*

What If...

There Is Not Enough Time? Send the questionnaire and scoring instructions to participants ahead of time. Ask participants to complete the questionnaire and to score their responses before coming to the session.

Participants Need Different Amounts of Time for Questionnaire Completion? Split the session into two parts. During the first part, give the introductory briefing and distribute the questionnaire. Ask participants to complete the questionnaire and to score the responses on their own. During the second session, help participants interpret their scores and explore the implications.

The Scoring Is Complex? Have participants complete the questionnaires ahead of time. Score the questionnaires or have them scored by experts. During the interactive lecture session, focus on helping participants interpret the scores and understand the implications.

Participants Are Afraid to Ask Questions? If they are worried about revealing their scores or response patterns, have them write the questions on unmarked index cards and drop them in a box.

There Is No Suitable Questionnaire? You can always find a questionnaire to suit your topic and participants if you search long enough. You can also create your own questionnaire.

Shouting Match

Interactive Lecture Design

This interactive lecture format is for exploring controversial topics and for dealing with misconceptions and prejudices. Don't even try Shouting Match unless you have the confidence and the competence to pull it off.

Key Feature

Organize participants into three teams and ask them to assume positive, negative, and neutral roles toward a controversial issue. Conduct an informal debate among the opposing teams and add your own comments.

When to Use This Format

Situations where Shouting Match may prove particularly efficacious include, but are not limited to, when:

- The instructional content is likely to arouse intense feelings.
- Participants have different opinions—and possible misconceptions—about the topic.
- You can present information and opinions in an unbiased manner.

Sample Topics

Topics for which Shouting Match would work well include

- affirmative action
- gun control legislation
- national health plan
- political correctness
- sexual harassment policies.

Supplies

You will need the following for this type of exercise:

- paper and pencil
- an attitude scale written on a flipchart page, transparency, or PowerPoint slide

- one or two copies of the scoring sheet.

Handout available in appendix

You'll also need a scoring sheet (handout 5-1), and you may want to distribute a summary of information and opinions at the end of the session.

Flow

Brief Participants. Introduce the issue and identify its major elements through an objective presentation. Write the issue or a proposition for a debate on a flipchart.

Sun's session is about a new pay-for-performance incentive system being implemented in the organization. Most participants have heard rumors about the system. She gives a two-minute presentation about important aspects of the system and tells the participants that they will be jointly exploring opinions and concerns about the system.

Establish a Baseline. Use the flipchart or project a slide to present the 9-point attitude scale:

1 = Very strongly disagree
2 = Strongly disagree
3 = Disagree
4 = Slightly disagree
5 = Neutral
6 = Slightly agree
7 = Agree
8 = Strongly agree
9 = Very strongly agree.

Repeat the topic or the proposition for a debate and emphasize that a 1 reflects the most negative position, 9 the most positive position, and 5 the neutral position. Ask each participant to write down any number from 1 to 9 to indicate his or her personal attitude. Assure participants that their attitudes will remain confidential.

Sun projects a transparency with the 9-point scale. She gives the participants some instructions and asks them to fold their piece of paper after they write their numbers.

Compute the Statistics. Collect the pieces of paper and ask one or two participants to tabulate the data and then compute the average using handout 5-1.

After the participants write their numbers, Sun collects the pieces of paper and gives them to Al, who happens to have a calculator. Al also gets a copy of the handout and goes to the back of the room to do the calculations.

Ask for Predictions. Ask everyone to think about the issue and about the probable range of reactions it would elicit among the people in the room. Ask participants to write a prediction of the average attitude score on the 9-point scale, correct to two decimal places. For example, participants should write 5.00 or 5.01 rather than 5.

While Al is working on his computations, Sun asks the other participants to write their predictions. She tells them to show their predictions to their neighbors.

Announce the Results. Tell the participants what the range and average scores were. Congratulate the person who made the closest prediction on his or her psychic ability.

After Al completes the computations, Sun gets the worksheet from him. She builds up some suspense by first asking the participants to guess the range of responses. Most people think the range is from 1 to 9. Checking the table, Sun announces that the real

range is from 1 to 8. She then asks the participants who predicted the average above 5 or below 2 to raise their hands. She informs them that their predictions are way off. Sun announces 3.27 is the average and congratulates Martha for her accurate guess of 3.25.

Form Three Teams. Use any convenient method for dividing participants into three teams. Ask the members of one team to assume that their attitude score for the topic is 1 (extremely negative), members of another team to assume that their attitude score is 9 (extremely positive), and members of the last team to assume that their attitude score is 5 (neutral). Ask the negative and the positive teams to spend the next five minutes making a list of arguments supporting their positions. During the same time, ask the neutral team to prepare a two-column list of both positive and negative arguments. Ask everyone to put aside their personal attitudes and seriously take on the role assigned to them while preparing the lists of arguments.

Sun asks the participants to count off by threes. She assembles all ones into the negative team, twos into the neutral team, and threes into the positive team. After giving the instructions and getting the teams to start listing their arguments, Sun walks around, listening to the conversations.

Conduct the Debate. Ask members of the positive team to stand on one side of the room and the negative team to stand on the opposite side. Ask the members of the neutral team to sit in the middle of the room. Explain the debate format: opposing teams will take turns making statements related to the issue; statements should be short five-second sound bites rather than elaborate explanations; statements don't need to be logical rebuttals of the previous statement made by the opposing team; participants can stray from their list of arguments; spontaneous comments are welcome; the debate ends when the pauses are too long.

Sun lines up the opposing teams on the opposite sides of the room and invites the negative team to start the debate. This team's spokesperson begins somewhat hesitantly saying that pay for performance is undemocratic. A member of the other team shouts that it is time for employees to be accountable for their productivity. A new spokesperson for the negative team counters with the argument that pay for performance is just a prelude to salary cuts. After about five minutes of increasingly louder arguments, Sun concludes the debate.

Identify the Winning Team. Ask members of the neutral team to evaluate the two opposing teams' performances and ask them to decide which team did a more credible job. Congratulate the winners.

Sun asks the members of the neutral team to close their eyes and vote if they think that the positive team's arguments were more credible. To confirm the result, she asks the team members to raise their hands if they think that the negative team's arguments were more credible. Sun notices that one of the neutral team members is abstaining, but she ignores this fact. She asks the neutral participants to open their eyes and announces that the negative team wins the debate. She leads a round of applause for this team.

Review the Neutral Team's List. Ask members of the neutral team to check their two-column list and read any arguments missed by the opposing teams.

Members of the neutral team announce that the other teams used most of their arguments. However, they point out that the negative team could have mentioned the enormous amount of paperwork required to support a pay-for-performance system.

Add Your Comments. It is now your turn to talk about the issue. Begin by briefly reviewing the positive and the negative arguments. If any of these reflect major misconceptions, correct them without appearing to be defensive. Present facts and alternative opinions.

Sun summarizes the research data on the effectiveness of pay-for-performance systems in large organizations. She lists the positive and negative outcomes and emphasizes the importance of long-term commitment to the new system. She identifies the major obstacles to the successful implementation of pay-for-performance systems.

Conduct a Q&A Session. Invite participants to ask questions related to different aspects of the topic. Respond to their questions clearing up any difficult subjects or misconceptions that might be tripping them up.

What If...
There Is Not Enough Time? Skip the attitude-testing phase. Move directly to team formation and preparation for the debate. Instead of conducting a debate in the suggested format, ask the three teams to read their lists of arguments. Follow up with your own comments.

Participants Don't Have Sufficient Background Knowledge? Make a presentation about the issue. Alternatively, show a videotape. You can also begin the session with a real debate between two people who hold opposite points of view.

There Are Too Many Participants? Divide participants into six or nine teams, with equal numbers of teams taking on the positive, negative, and neutral roles. Then randomly select one representative from each team to take part in the debate.

The Issue Is Very Controversial? Conduct the session with small groups. Limit the teams to reading their lists of arguments.

You Have Strong Opinions About the Issue? Choose a neutral facilitator to conduct the activity. Keep your opinions to yourself. Remember that this interactive lecture format is for sharing information and opinions and not for advocating your position.

Participants Have Major Misconceptions? If you are working for a client and if the employees refuse to believe the facts and figures, you have brought into the open a major credibility problem. Schedule a follow-up session in which the top management from your client's organization can address the issue.

Participants Are Biased? If the members of the opposing teams claim that they are unable to think of any arguments to support the position assigned to them, work with the team and offer relevant suggestions. Persuade them to get into the spirit of role playing.

Concluding Thoughts

Here are some notes from the field about this type of interactive lecture:

●◆ Participants everywhere enjoy FAQs and Fakes because it offers them an opportunity to fool their fellow participants and show off their ability to be an imposter. Sometimes the fake responses are so interesting and credible that I have to remind everyone to focus on the correct information.

●◆ I use Questionnaire Analysis with about 10 different personality-type instruments such as Myers-Briggs Type Indicator (MBTI) assessment. This format may not as enjoyable as the others in this chapter, but participants are totally absorbed because it is all about them. You need to do your homework and become a qualified administrator of the tests to ensure the validity and reliability of the information given to participants.

●◆ Shouting Match uses a single item to effectively tap into participants' reactions to a controversial topic. Although this format appears to be a simple one, I am always amazed by the breadth of positive and negative points generated by the participants and the depth of their discussion.

Random assignment of "attitudes" to the three teams prevents personal attacks and polarized arguments. In using this format, I have to make sure that I can remain neutral and limit my presentation to factual information rather than biased opinions.

●◆ Confusion is different from the other formats in this chapter because the lecture precedes the test. Nevertheless, the test is primarily used for probing and pinpointing participants' difficulties. In using this approach, I have to constantly limit myself to the clarification of participants' confusion rather than using the questions as an invitation to undertake another data-dump lecture.

In assessment-based interactive lectures, participants indirectly control the scope and sequence of your lecture presentation through their responses to a test, questionnaire, or attitude scale. What do you think would happen if you let participants directly control your presentation (without having to respond to a test or some other instrument)? In the next chapter, we explore five different interactive lecture formats in which direct participant control determines your presentation strategy.

Participant Control

Giving control over to the participants encourages them to tell you *what* they want to learn and, to some extent, *how* they want to learn. Sometimes, you may have to establish the context by making an initial presentation and then proceeding to spend most of your time responding to the audience's learning choices.

The five methods covered in this chapter are these:

- *Brainstorm:* Use this method for open-ended discussion when the lecture topic is informational or conceptual.
- *Fishbowl:* This format allows participants to learn by observing a coaching session.
- *Item List:* This method of lecture depends on participants choosing items to have explained in detail.
- *Press Conference:* This interactive lecture method relies on the participants to grill an expert in a simulated press conference environment.
- *Selected Questions:* This game allows participants to generate questions before a lecture and you answer questions beginning with the top ones.

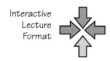

Brainstorm

Brainstorm works effectively with adult learners who have rich and diverse backgrounds. I often use this method to provide an introduction to lecture games.

Key Feature

The presenter conducts a brainstorming session on an open-ended question, contributing his or her own ideas whenever appropriate. (You may wish to review handout 2-2 in the appendix.) After brainstorming, the presenter derives some general principles on the topic and corrects any misconceptions.

When to Use This Game

Situations under which the implementation of this method would be most efficacious include when:

- The instructional content is primarily informational or conceptual, or if the content involves analyzing and solving a problem.
- Participants have relevant background experiences and opinions—including misconceptions and prejudices.
- You have established enough credibility with participants.

Sample Topics

Topics similar to the ones listed below would be successful with the Brainstorm learning method:

- cultural characteristics of the Japanese
- customer service
- gender differences in the workplace
- long-distance networking
- waste reduction in the workplace.

Equipment

A flipchart and markers are required for this activity. In addition, you will need to distribute to the participants a handout that has a summary of important points.

Flow

Introduce the Topic and Format. Specify the scope of the presentation and inform participants about the Brainstorm approach. If necessary, explain briefly the ground rules.

Leif begins by telling the group that his presentation is about lectures. However, instead of lecturing about lectures, he is going to conduct a Brainstorm session. Because everyone in the audience has sat through several lectures and probably has some experience in giving them, there should not be any major difficulty in participating in the Brainstorm session.

Present the Brainstorming Task. Ask a question that is broad enough to elicit responses.

Leif's prompting question is: "From the trainer's perspective, what are the advantages of using the lecture method?" He uses a transparency and projects this question on the overhead screen and asks participants to spend a couple of minutes silently jotting down their responses on a piece of paper. Then Leif invites them to yell out their answers.

Record Ideas on the Flipchart. Paraphrase the responses and quickly jot them down.

Nicole, one of the participants, suggests that most trainers use lectures because it makes them feel important. Leif paraphrases her response as "ego trip." Harley suggests that lectures permit the trainer to maintain control over the training event. Leif writes down "control." Other points include efficiency, ease of preparation, and ignorance of other training methods.

Make Comments. Whenever there is a lull in the responses, comment on the items on the flipchart. Present supporting or challenging data. Identify any discrepancies and provide suitable explanations.

Commenting on the idea of control, Leif suggests in tongue-in-cheek fashion that personality studies indicate that next to police officers, trainers have the highest need for control. Leif goes on to challenge the idea that lectures are easy to prepare by pointing out that some lecturers spend dozens of hours to prepare a 30-minute presentation.

Correct Misconceptions. When the Brainstorm ends, be sure to present opposing points of view.

Leif reviews the list on the flipchart and comments that most of the advantages of the lecture method appear to be shallow and self-serving. He points out that the method does have some genuine advantages, especially when used by an inspiring and knowledgeable presenter.

Repeat the Process. Suggest other related topics to brainstorm. Use the same procedure to process participants' responses.

Leif now asks the group to brainstorm these questions one at a time:

> I am a great believer in letting the inmates run the asylum. Instead of conducting expensive and extensive audience analysis prior to the lecture, I choose to give the control to the participants and let them dictate the scope and sequence of my lecture.

- *From the learner's perspective, what are the advantages of the lecture method?*
- *What are the major disadvantages of the lecture method?*
- *What can you do to reduce the disadvantages and increase the advantages of the lecture method?*

Participants point out that the lecture method provides comfort and security to the learners. They identify the lack of feedback as a major disadvantage and suggest strategies for inserting dialogs within a lecture to improve its effectiveness.

Summarize the Major Points. Identify patterns among these ideas. Reemphasize the importance of maintaining a balance between opposing points of view. You should now distribute the handout you prepared and discuss major differences between the ideas listed on it and the ideas generated by the participants.

Leif's summary is brief because he has already covered most of the points during the lulls in the brainstorming sessions. He distributes copies of a handout that lists important points and asks participants to spend a few minutes comparing the handout with the flipchart records of their responses. Leif briefly discusses any major differences.

A lecturer looked up from his notes and was dismayed to see that one of the participants was sound asleep. Sternly, he called out to the woman sitting next to the snoring fellow, "Hey, poke that guy and wake him up!" "Why should I?" she asked. "You're the one who put him to sleep!"

What If...

There Is Not Enough Time? Conduct fewer brainstorming sessions. Quickly elicit participants' ideas without writing them down. Treat some of the brainstorming questions as rhetorical.

There Are Too Many Participants? Write down audience inputs on a blank transparency and project them on the screen. Use a couple of volunteers from the audience to work with two different overhead projectors while you encourage the participants.

Participants Do Not Come Up With Any Ideas? Prompt them by listing a few sample responses. As an alternative, plant some suggested responses with confederates in the audience. Ask participants to find a partner and collaborate in coming up with responses.

Participants Have Incorrect or Prejudiced Ideas? These ideas provide valuable input. Use them to stimulate discussion, and challenge the participants with data to remove the misconceptions and prejudices.

Participants Overlook Critical Ideas? Remember: You, too, can play. If nobody brings up a critical idea, point out that some previous groups suggested the missing idea.

You Are Worried About Losing Your Credibility? Impress them with your periodic corrections and comments and with the final handout. If you are conscientious in creating the handout, learners will appreciate your valuable reference material.

Fishbowl

People learn by watching others learn. With the Fishbowl learning format, participants learn by observing a coaching session.

Key Feature

You conduct a one-on-one coaching session in the middle of the room (the Fishbowl). Other participants observe and participate vicariously.

When to Use This Format

Use this format when:

- Instructional content involves information, procedures, concepts, or principles.
- Participants are capable of participating in a one-on-one coaching session without spectators distracting them.
- You can conduct a coaching session without becoming self-conscious about several others observing you.

Sample Topics

Fishbowl has proven to be most beneficial when used to deal with such topics as:

- ways to deal with older customers
- how to design a form
- how to prepare a frequency table
- how to write advertisement copy
- sexual discrimination in the workplace
- types of interview questions.

Supplies and Equipment

To conduct Fishbowl, you must provide job aids and summaries of the instructional topic to the participants in your session. The equipment necessary includes an overhead projector and a screen or a white wall on which to project the image.

Flow

Prepare for the Presentation. Be sure that you have a full set of appropriate examples and practice materials.

Kate is making a presentation on how to prepare a Pareto chart. She makes copies of a checklist that outlines the step-by-step procedure. She also creates step-by-step examples of preparing a Pareto chart. She converts them into transparencies because she wants everyone in the group to see what she is showing the learner.

Arrange the Facilities for Maximum Visibility. Set up a table and a couple of chairs in the middle of the room. Invite participants to gather around the table to watch the action in the Fishbowl. If the group is large, use a microphone and put your samples on transparencies projected on a screen so that everyone can see them. Afterward, you should distribute copies of the handout, making sure that everyone gets one.

Because of the small number of participants, Kate invites them to stand around the table and observe the coaching procedure. She sets up an overhead projector at the tabletop level and places the learner's chair so that it faces the screen. Right after, Kate distributes copies of the checklist and the step-by-step examples of creating two different Pareto charts.

Select Your First Candidate. You can avoid unpleasant surprises by previously informing a participant that you will select him or her. Alternatively, if you think any member of the group can play the role easily, you may select a random participant.

Before distributing the handouts, Kate placed a check mark on one of them. She asks the person with the check mark, Jack, to be the first learner.

Explain What You and the Participants Will Be Doing.

You are going to coach the selected student. You want the other participants to participate vicariously in the process by imagining themselves seated in the learner's chair. From time to time, you will switch learners so someone else is in the Fishbowl.

Kate makes her introductory remarks. She also asks the participants to look at the screen on which she will project all her written demonstrations.

Begin the Coaching Session.

Start with a conversation in which you orient the student to the topic, the objectives, and the materials.

Kate makes sure that Jack is comfortable. She shows him a frequency table and a final Pareto chart. She briefly explains the powerful uses of the Pareto chart. Kate asks Jack about his responsibilities and identifies several areas where Pareto charts could be useful. She then shows Jack and the others a checklist on how to construct a Pareto chart.

Give a Demonstration.

Present background information and principles. Make a clear presentation and invite the learner to ask questions and to seek clarification whenever he or she wants.

Kate demonstrates how to convert a frequency table into a cumulative table, using a transparency and a felt-tipped pen. She then gets ready to demonstrate the actual drawing of the Pareto chart.

Ask Questions.

Require the participant to demonstrate what he or she has learned.

Kate gives Jack another frequency table and asks him to apply the procedure and prepare a cumulative table. Kate suggests that the other participants follow along. As Jack creates a table on a blank transparency, Kate gives appropriate guidance and feedback.

Switch the Active Participant.

You can do this even in the middle of a step. Just ask someone to come up and replace your first volunteer and repeat the same procedures until the topic is completely covered.

Kate asks Ruth to come up and take Jack's place. Kate lets Ruth complete the rest of the cumulative table, after which Kate explains how to draw the Pareto chart. She asks Ruth to get started on making a Pareto chart using the table she had created earlier. After the first couple of steps, Kate replaces Ruth with Alima.

Respond to Questions.

At the conclusion of the coaching session, ask participants if they have any questions. Give all participants additional practice exercises.

A couple of participants ask questions about modifying some of the steps. Kate agrees that a person will get the same results whether cumulative percentages or frequencies are used for constructing the Pareto chart. She strongly recommends, however, that participants stick with the cumulative frequencies. Kate gives participants another frequency table and asks them to construct a Pareto chart. While the participants work independently, she walks around, helping people as they require.

What If...

There Is Not Enough Time? Speed up your demonstration and get your student applying the procedure as quickly as possible. Stay with the same person the entire coaching session. Have participants complete the final practice exercise as a homework assignment.

Your Topic Is Complex? Divide your topic into two or more parts and demonstrate and coach different parts during different sessions.

Your Learner Has Stage Fright? Avoid this possibility by asking for a volunteer to be in the Fishbowl. Reassure the person that he or she will not have to do anything embarrassing.

Nobody Volunteers? Avoid this possibility by selecting a participant ahead of time. Rehearse the Fishbowl coaching session with this participant.

Item List

Some presentations involve a list of items such as principles, facts, rules, guidelines, suggestions, advantages, myths, opinions, characteristics, or tips. The Item List format is especially effective for such presentations.

Key Feature

Participants review a list of items and select a few for you to explain in detail. They also select other items for discussion and debate.

When to Use This Format

I recommend you use Item List if the following situations match your lecture circumstances:

Handout
available in
appendix

- You can organize the instructional content into a list of items.
- Participants can take charge of controlling your presentation.
- You can deal with participants' preferences in a flexible manner.

Sample Topics

Topics for which Item List works well include, but are by no means limited to:

- basic principles of message design
- gender differences in communication styles
- guidelines for conducting a workshop
- negotiation principles
- tips for training diverse work groups
- trends in performance technology.

Handouts

Each participant should be provided the list of items that you will be discussing over the course of your interactive lecture.

Flow

Brief the Participants. Introduce the instructional topic and explain that you will provide a list of items related to the topic and let participants select which items they would like you to discuss in detail. Have participants review and analyze the handout. Give them a couple of minutes to study the handout independently, underline key words, and scribble questions in the margins.

Vartan's session is on business reengineering, and he is presenting it to a group of human resources specialists. He begins with a short introduction to define the concept and then distributes a one-page handout containing 17 reengineering rules (handout 6-1).

Ginny reviews the handout and finds many of the rules to be self-explanatory. She places a check mark in front of them. She places question marks in front of a couple that she does not understand. She reads the list again and begins to doodle absent-mindedly all over the page.

Form Partnerships. Ask participants to pair up with someone seated nearby. Each pair should identify items that require more explanation and arrange these items in order of priority. Spend about two minutes on this activity.

Ginny and Manuel partner up and compare lists. They agree that they would like to find out what rule 5 on distributive computing is all about. They also want clarification of the functional departments and process teams mentioned in rule 13. Manuel wants an explanation of the difference between education and training in rule 16, but Ginny says that she can explain that.

Clarify the Items. Ask a volunteer to identify the first item that needs clarification. Provide a brief and clear explanation, using examples whenever possible. Try not to regress into lecture mode. Once you have clarified this item, ask for another volunteer and another item. Continue with explanations of different items until participants run out of requests.

Ginny is the first volunteer. She wants rule 5 clarified. Vartan explains that standardizing certain procedures in an organization has major advantages. For example, a centralized training curriculum can save developmental costs and ensure consistent performance among the employees in different departments. At the same time, decentralizing certain procedures may provide greater flexibility to different units of the organization.

For example, branch offices should determine the pay scale depending on the local cost of living. An organization needs an appropriate mix of centralized and localized standards. As an example, Vartan suggests that the organization should design software at the corporate headquarters but permit suitable modifications at the local branches.

Ask for Supporting Comments. Ask the partners to review the list and to select one or more items with which they agree wholeheartedly and about which they have some personal experience. Ask for a volunteer who can explain an item and can provide anecdotes from personal experience.

Cece selects rule 4, which exhorts people not to be cheap. She explains that it is important to "put your money where your mouth is" if the top management wants to bring about effective changes. She recounts the half-hearted attempt by people in her previous company to provide computers to all managers. After buying powerful computers equipped with fast Pentium processors, management decided to save money by equipping these computers with inexpensive 120-megabyte hard drives. Most managers soon ran out of storage space and gave up attempts at serious computing when they learned that there was no budget for expanding their hard drives. Cece thought that by denying an extra 10 percent expenditure, the company lost the value of its investment in the computers. Vartan calls the story an excellent example of rule 4 being violated.

Ask for Challenges. Ask the partners to review the list again and to identify one or more items they would like to challenge. Ask for a volunteer and conduct a good-natured debate with this person. If no one wants to challenge you, play devil's advocate and challenge one of the items yourself. Ask a volunteer to defend the item during a friendly debate. At the end of the debate, comment on the limitations of the item.

Beth and Lana want to challenge rule 10, which recommends radical changes over continuous improvement. Lana volunteers to debate with Vartan and complains that radical changes may result in throwing out the baby with the bath water. Also, such changes are likely to produce enormous resistance among the employees. Vartan responds by pointing out that minor adjustments rarely lead to significant improvements in productivity. They usually involve a few adjustments in the steps of a process when it would be better to discard the whole process. In addition, continuous improvement cannot keep pace with technological breakthroughs. Vartan offered an example, saying that no amount of improvement in typewriters could have matched the quantum gains achieved through word-processing software. Lana interrupts and accuses Vartan of using a limited set of examples, ones that have nothing to do with day-to-day corporate activities. She points out that after the dramatic introduction of word processors, the improvements in the field have been gradual and continuous.

After several other attacks and retorts, Vartan concedes that perhaps both reengineering and continuous improvement have advantages in different situations.

Use Additional Activities. Require partners to process the Item List in different ways. For example, ask them to identify situations to which different items apply or organize the items in logical categories, or to add to the list.

Vartan asks the partners to decide which three items they would like to drop from the Item List. He asks Peter and Ginny for their choices and justifications. After listening to Peter and Ginny, Vartan asks the participants who have dissenting opinions to make their case.

Conclude the Session. Spend the last five minutes inviting questions and comments from participants. Respond to questions and react to comments.

During the concluding period, participants ask half a dozen questions (example: What is a good book about reengineering?), and Vartan provides brief answers. Myron says that although he intellectually understands the reengineering concept, he is somewhat anxious about the recommendations. Vartan responds that he is not pushing reengineering as a cure for every problem. He merely recommends that the participants think about the rules, talk about them with their colleagues, and make their own decisions.

What If...

There Is Not Enough Time? Concentrate on clarifying the items selected by the partners. Add the other types of activities only if time permits.

Nobody Volunteers? Randomly select a pair of partners and persuade the pair to participate in the first activity. Continue random selections unless a participant volunteers.

The Same Participant Keeps Volunteering? Establish a rule that no one should volunteer more than once.

There Are Very Few Participants? Organize them into pairs of partners and then have the pairs take turns.

There Are Too Many Items on Your Item List? Divide the list into two or more logical sections and conduct an interactive lecture session with each section.

Press Conference

This is one of the first interactive lecture formats I developed—perhaps in a fit of megalomania. During the past 20 years, many people have used Press Conference successfully for training and for disseminating information.

Key Features

Organize participants into teams and ask them to create and organize questions for grilling an expert in a simulated press conference.

When to Use This Format

Lecturers have found Press Conference to be most helpful under the following circumstances:

- The instructional content is primarily factual—such as product specifications—or informational—such as new policies and procedures.

- Participants know enough about the topic to ask intelligent questions as in the case of a technical update or when they have enough self-interest to ask relevant questions as in the case of a new policy.

- You have enough expertise and experience in the subject to handle a variety of questions and to think on your feet.

Sample Topics

Subjects similar to those listed below work especially well with the fundamentals covered in Press Conference:

- the Americans With Disabilities Act
- introduction to business reengineering

- marketing in Pacific Rim nations
- new-hire orientation
- new-product training
- overview of promotion policies.

Supplies

All you need to implement this method is some index cards.

Flow

Present an Overview. Briefly introduce the content you will be covering in your session to the participants. Keep it short (less than two minutes). Provide a rationale for the session. Identify the key objectives and present an outline of major topics.

> *David's session is on sexual harassment. He briefly explains why this is an important topic for everybody in the organization and its implications for personal and professional conduct. He suggests dividing the subject area into four major topics, which he numbers on a flipchart: the definition of sexual harassment, the victim's rights, the accused person's rights, and organizational policy.*

Generate Questions. Distribute index cards to participants and ask them to write at least one question on each topic related to the presentation. They should record the topic number on a line above each question.

> *David distributes different colored index cards to each participant. He asks them to write a question related to the definition of sexual harassment on the green card, one related to the victim's rights on the blue card, one related to the accused person's rights on the orange card, and one related to the organizational policy on the yellow*

card. He invites people to ask for more cards of any color if they want to write additional questions. He also announces a two-minute time limit.

Organize the Teams. After collecting the cards, divide participants into as many teams as there are topics. Ask the teams to sit together at tables.

After two minutes, David asks the participants to stop writing after they complete the question they're working on. He collects the cards and then asks the participants to organize into four teams of approximately equal size. David separates the question cards according to their color.

Teams Organize Their Questions. Give each team a different set of cards, and ask members to review the questions, to eliminate duplicate or trivial questions, and to arrange the remaining questions in a logical order. Announce a suitable time limit.

David distributes the cards to the four teams. Each team reviews and organizes its set in slightly different ways. Steve's team spreads out the cards on the table. Each person picks a card, silently reads the question, and places it near another card to which it is related. John's team begins by creating a classification scheme even before looking at the cards. Susan's team distributes packets of cards to different members, who then take turns reading the question aloud and discussing where it should be placed. David reviews his notes and walks around listening to different discussions.

Conduct the Press Conference. Explain that you will play the role of an expert conducting a Press Conference. Select one of the teams to role play a group of reporters, using their cards to ask you questions for

10 minutes. While you answer these questions, all participants should take careful notes because a follow-up activity will involve the information you present.

David puts on a pair of fake glasses, stands behind a podium, and introduces himself as Dr. Guthro, a nationally recognized authority on sexual harassment. He randomly selects the green team that has the questions dealing with definitional issues to be the first group of reporters. He starts a timer. The green team members spend a few moments organizing themselves. Then one of the team members reads a question about a manager touching a female employee in a friendly fashion without any ulterior motive. Dr. Guthro explains the difference between intent and impact of actions in a cross-gender interaction.

The team members continue with additional questions, including some obviously created to follow up David's earlier responses. The timer goes off after 10 minutes, and David hurriedly completes his response and concludes the first press conference.

Process the Information. Ask members of each team (including the team that asked the questions) to compare notes and to identify what they consider the two most important pieces of information in your answers. Give the teams three minutes to contemplate and complete this exercise.

David gives the instructions and sets his timer for three minutes. While the teams are discussing their notes, he flips through his notes about the rights of a person accused of sexually harassing an employee.

Teams Report Out. Ask a representative from each team to read or state what team members consider the two most important pieces of information. Listen carefully to each report, and make any appropriate comments.

David selects the teams at random and asks them for their reports. All four teams agree that one of the most important pieces of information is that there are different types of sexual harassment.

Repeat the Press Conference Session. Continue with more rounds of the Press Conference, giving each team an opportunity to ask its questions. Follow up each round with teams identifying the two most important pieces of information related to that topic.

Conclude the Activity. After the last round of team reports, present any additional information that participants should know. Invite individual participants to ask questions regarding any aspect of the topic about which they are concerned or curious.

During his concluding presentation, David shares his expectation that laws and policies related to sexual harassment will keep pace with changes in social values.

What If...

There Is Not Enough Time? Eliminate the step during which team members organize and edit the questions; give each team its cards and select one team to begin the questioning. Eliminate the team review of the responses and identification of the two important pieces of information. Ask participants to come to the session with prepared questions. Reduce each Press Conference to five minutes—or to three questions.

Participants Don't Ask Important Questions? Prepare your own questions and add them to participants' cards when you distribute them to different teams. After the last round of the Press Conference, tell participants that you are going to ask yourself some more questions and answer them.

Many Questions Are Left Unanswered? Collect the unanswered questions and prepare a handout with the answers to be distributed as a follow-up activity.

Interactive
Lecture
Format

Selected Questions

This interactive lecture format requires that audience members take on additional responsibilities to increase their ownership of the material being presented.

Key Feature

Preview a list of questions generated before the presentation, remove all duplicates, and arrange them in random order. Begin your presentation by answering the question selected by most participants. Repeat the process by responding to popular questions successively selected by the listeners.

When to Use This Format

Times when this method of conducting interactive lectures proves especially efficacious include the following:

- Your audience members represent different areas of interest and levels of knowledge.
- Your audience members have equal opportunity to contribute questions.
- The presentation requires a broad survey of a topical area.
- You are willing to relinquish control of the session to the participants.

Handout available in appendix

Sample Topics

The list below contains examples of topics that work well for Selected Questions:

- performance improvement
- emotional intelligence
- motivation
- conflict management
- negotiation
- cross-cultural communication.

Handout

You must provide a list of prepared (and randomly arranged) questions from which your lecture topics will be chosen.

Preparation

Make the List. Ask the session organizer to type up the questions from audience members. Remove all duplicates and sort the list alphabetically to ensure a random sequence. Enumerate the list and review the questions to get a feel for the audience's level of interest and knowledge.

A group of public managers invites Jin to talk to them about new principles and procedures related to leadership. He works with the conference organizers to encourage participants to submit questions to him in advance by email. Jin reviews the 23 questions that the participants would like to have addressed, removes three duplicate questions, arranges the remaining questions in alphabetical order, and produces a handout to be given to participants in his session (handout 6-2).

Flow

Pass Out the Handout. Give a copy of the list of questions you made in preparation for this lecture to each participant.

Explain Your Plan and Its Logic. Point out that it is neither feasible nor desirable to respond to all the questions listed. Instead of arbitrarily deciding which questions to answer, you are going to entrust the responsibility to a group of experts: members of the audience. Although this process requires time, it is a worthwhile investment that will ensure return of relevance to participants. Ask participants to review the questions and invite them to eliminate these categories:

- rhetorical questions for which the answer is obvious
- smart-alecky questions that are designed to show off the questioner's sophistication
- trivial questions that do not add value to the listeners
- factual questions that are answered in reference books
- idiosyncratic questions that are relevant to only a few individuals.

Pause for a few minutes while participants complete this task.

Jin has printed this list of categories immediately after the list of questions, making it easier for participants to undertake the elimination task.

Identify the First Question.

After a suitable pause, ask participants to review remaining questions and independently select the question they would like to have answered first. This should be a basic question that will contribute to a better understanding of subsequent questions.

Lucy, one of the audience members, selects question 6 about gender differences in leadership.

Conduct an Informal Poll.

Ask participants to shout out the identifying number of the question with which they want to start the lecture. Encourage participants with the same preferences to repeat shouted numbers. Listen to the shouted numbers and identify the one that is most loudly or frequently shouted.

Poor Lucy's shouts for number 6 are drowned out by the yelling of other

My friend Mike Molenda frequently invites me to address his group of graduate students. A couple of days before the session, he sends me a list of questions collected from people who plan to attend. This list provides valuable information about the needs of the audience. I review, organize, and sequence these questions. I realize, however, that this organization is likely to reflect my priorities rather than the priorities of the audience. To avoid this—and to justify my laziness—I developed the Selected Questions method.

numbers. Jin is not sure, but he thinks that the loudest shout was for question 9.

Respond to the Question.

Make a succinct presentation, and encourage participants to listen carefully and to take notes.

Jin checks his list of questions and gives his response: The need for technical expertise decreases and the need for interpersonal and conceptual expertise increases as one progresses through the leadership hierarchy. He explains that a front-line supervisor should demonstrate technical expertise but a senior executive should be more fluent with interpersonal and conceptual skills. He continues his explanation for about five minutes.

Pause for Reflection.

After your response, ask participants to individually jot down a single sentence that captures and summarizes the most important point from your presentation.

During the pause, instead of writing a sentence, Lucy draws a simple chart that helps her organize the major points of different leadership categories and different types of expertise.

Identify the Next Question. Ask participants to review other questions. Point out that the importance of specific questions might have increased or decreased because of the key points covered in the lecture thus far. Repeat the earlier informal polling to identify the next question you will answer. As before, choose the question that seems to be in the highest demand and give a brief lecture on the question and its subtopics. After answering the second question, pause for personalized summaries. Repeat this process as time allows.

> *Finally, during the fifth round, Lucy is able to convince a group of participants seated near her to call out for question 6 (Does gender play a role in leadership?) very loudly.*
>
> *Jin responds by identifying some obvious differences in values of men and women leaders (such as women tend to encourage collaboration while men tend to encourage competition). He also points out several similarities between genders and predicts that androgynous leaders who combine male and female values will be in great demand in the future.*

Generate More Questions. Set aside the last five minutes for participants to write questions that should have been in the original list but were not. Collect these questions and briefly answer one or two. Tell participants that you will post brief answers to the remaining questions on your Website if such resources are at your disposal. Alternatively, offer to answer the remaining questions during your next visit to that lecture arena.

> *Jin is only able to respond to a couple of these questions before time is up. He promises the participants that he will post the answers to the remaining questions on his Website in weekly installments.*

What If...

There Are Too Many Questions From the Audience? Randomly select about 15 questions for your list. Explain that the list contains only a representative sample.

Some Critical Questions Are Omitted? This feeling is usually due to megalomania on your part. Add your critical questions to the list. Confess to participants that you have added a few questions but do not identify them. (It serves you right if your questions get eliminated or ignored by participants!)

Questions Weren't Collected From Participants in Advance? Prepare your own list and use it instead. Be sure to include some naïve, trivial, redundant, and smart-alecky questions.

You Don't Want to Type All the Questions? Ask the organizer to type them and send you a word-processed document or have them emailed from the participants directly to you. Cut and paste the questions into a word-processed document. You can create and modify the list any way you want.

Concluding Thoughts

My favorite interactive lecture strategies involve participant control. I use this type of lectures frequently as you can see from these real-world examples of my training sessions during the past 30 days:

- People from around the world know how to participate in brainstorming sessions, and so I have no trouble with using the Brainstorm format. I used this approach during a training session on customer service and I was amazed at the variety of strategies suggested by participants. I had no trouble aligning their inputs with my "official" list.

- I conducted a session on financial analysis and used the Fishbowl format to explain the procedure for computing the net present value. (Yes, it is a boring topic.) All participants had a step-by-step checklist and a laptop loaded with financial analysis software program. I brought Steve, one of the participants, to the front of the room and worked through the procedure on a laptop that was attached to an LCD projector. Other participants had no difficulty following along. After a few steps through the procedure, I tried to replace Steve with Supriya, but Steve was having so much fun that he refused to go back! It took me a few minutes to convince Steve that he can still continue working through the other steps from his original seat in the classroom.

- I conducted a training session on success factors for virtual teams using the Item List format. My list contained 12 items collected from a host of books on the topic. The first item that was selected by participants

dealt with gaining trust among the members of a virtual team. I explained major differences between trust in face-to-face teams and virtual teams. Many participants were eager to support my explanation with their "betrayal" experiences when they did not receive a reply to their urgent email notes.

- In Zurich, I had a Swiss expert present his research findings related to high-performing intercultural teams. I acted as his host and conducted a Press Conference session in which he was the expert. The main difficulty I had was to control the researcher's enthusiasm and limit him to a short overview at the beginning. I also had to have an intelligent conversation with him while participants collected and edited the questions. In the end, however, everyone—including the researcher—was happy with the outcomes of the session.

- I made a guest appearance at the regular monthly meeting of the Birmingham, Alabama, ASTD chapter. The program chair collected a list of questions (about training games and simulations) from the participants who attended the previous meeting. This enabled me to conduct an effective and engaging session using the Selected Questions format.

Even when we give up control to participants, we still play the key role in making lecture presentations. What would happen if we co-opted the participants to take on the role of the trainer and make presentations to each other? The next chapter explores two interactive lecture formats related to the powerful technique of peer teaching.

Teamwork

From ancient times, people have figured out that the best way to learn something is to teach it to others. Impressive data from recent experimental research on collaborative learning supports this principle.

In a multilevel coaching exercise, you teach different steps in a procedure—or different concepts related to a topic—to different groups of participants. You then reorganize the groups into teams in which at least one person knows each step or concept, and challenge the teams to solve problems collaboratively. In the process of solving problems, team members teach each other and end up mastering all the steps—or concepts. This chapter includes two methods:

- *Multilevel Coaching:* This game exploits the fact that coaching others is an effective way to learn a skill.
- *Team Teaching:* This game allows participants to be both lecturer and participant.

Multilevel Coaching

Technical training frequently involves manual skills such as operating a lathe, replacing a fuse, taking blood pressure, cleaning a carburetor, using a computer mouse, or transferring digital images to a laptop computer. Mastery of these skills requires individual demonstration and coaching. In Multilevel Coaching (MLC), all participants receive individual attention. The game exploits the fact that coaching others is an effective way to learn a skill.

Key Feature

Unlike other interactive lecture formats, not everyone participates in MLC at the same time. The activity begins with a few individuals learning the skill and then teaching other participants on a one-on-one basis. The activity begins slowly and gradually speeds up to include everyone. MLC is best conducted over a period of hours or days.

When to Use This Format

I recommend you use MLC under the following conditions:

- The instructional content is primarily a physical skill.
- Participants have the commitment and patience to teach (and learn from) each other.
- You have access to enough pieces of the required supplies and equipment.

Sample Topics

Topics similar to ones listed below will benefit from the use of MLC:

- unarmed combat
- skiing
- yoga postures
- juggling
- performing magic tricks with playing cards
- conversational Japanese.

Supplies

You will need to bring a checklist summarizing the steps and any supplies or equipment required for performing the task to be learned.

Preparation

Prepare a Job Aid. Create a checklist that explains each step in the procedure. Use this as a supplementary reference material as you demonstrate and explain the skill.

> *During a recent three-day conference on health and safety, Jennifer is asked to teach participants how to perform the Heimlich maneuver. She finds copies of an illustrated brochure that describes the procedure.*

Assemble the Supplies. Collect any materials or equipment required for performing the procedure.

Flow

Recruit and Train Leaders. Identify four participants from the group as the leaders. Train them by providing a complete demonstration, incorporating the job aid. Ask the leaders to demonstrate their mastery of the procedure and give constructive feedback. Coach the leaders until they reach a high level of mastery.

> *Jennifer's four leaders are Steve, Ronaldo, Judee, and Seethal. Jennifer recruits them Monday morning at the conference desk. After about 30 minutes of demonstration and practice, they all achieve a high level of mastery.*

Explain the MLC Procedure to the Leaders. Appoint two leaders as captains of the Red Team and the other two as captains of the Blue Team (or, to promote competitive spirit, you can have the teams come up with their own names). Explain the following procedure using your own words:

- Your goal is to recruit and train as many of the other participants as possible. However, you can train only one person at a time.
- Whenever you feel confident about your trainee's skill level, find a certified member of the other team. In the beginning, the four of you are the only certified people. Ask the certified person from the other team to be a performance tester.
- The tester will observe the trainee as he or she demonstrates the skill. This tester will either pass your trainee or give specific feedback about the trainee's deficits.
- If the trainee fails, provide additional coaching to improve his or her skill level. Request another performance test from the same tester or from any other certified member of the other team.
- If the trainee passes, he or she becomes a certified member of your team.
- All certified participants can recruit others and train them, always on an individual basis.
- From time to time, a certified member of the other team may bring a new trainee to you for performance testing. Ask the trainee to demonstrate the skill and observe the performance carefully. Decide whether to pass or fail this trainee. In the latter case, provide specific feedback about what was missing in the trainee's performance.

- You and all other certified members of your team can recruit and train several other participants. However, you should work with an individual participant until he or she is tested and certified.

Jennifer tells her four leaders to combine their training and coaching among all other conference activities. She also instructs them to attend the final Heimlich session from 2:00 p.m. to 3:00 p.m. on Wednesday.

Monitor the Activity. Send the team leaders on their way. Keep track of what is happening with the participants but do not interfere.

During the next two days, Jennifer interviews the four leaders and observes them in action.

Conclude the Activity. Conduct a general meeting, and ask the certified members of both teams to assemble at different sides of the room. Do a rapid body count to identify the winning team. Congratulate the winners and thank all participants for the mutual teaching and learning experience. Conduct a quick debriefing and answer any questions. Encourage all participants to continue spreading the skill among their friends, family members, and co-workers when they return home.

Jennifer conducts her final session on Wednesday afternoon. The Blue Team wins with 37 certified members (in comparison with 23 certified members in the Red Team). Jennifer invites a few representatives from each team to come up to the stage and demonstrate their newly acquired skills. After a question-and-answer session, she sends out all participants to make the world a safer place for choking victims.

Do you know the definition of "lecture"? It is the most efficient method for transferring the content from the instructor's notes to the trainees' notebooks—without passing through either person's brain.

What If...

There Is Not Enough Time or Too Many Participants? Increase the number of teams and team leaders. Permit certified members to train small groups of (up to four) participants at a time.

There Are Too Few Participants? Have only one leader for each of the two teams, and you can fill the role of performance tester for all learners.

There Are Insufficient Supplies? Use a sign-up sheet for scheduling the use of equipment. Allow ample time before the beginning of MLC and the general meeting session.

There Is Too Much Competition? Instead of setting up different teams to compete against each other, give the leaders a time limit for bringing all participants up to speed.

You Are Worried About Poor Quality? Use an objective checklist for rating the test performance. Train a separate group of participants to administer the performance test. Alternatively, use outside experts to conduct the test and certify the participants.

Some Participants Are Not Certified by the End of the Activity? Prevent this from happening by allocating sufficient time and by training a larger initial group of team leaders. If a small number of participants is left out at the end of the activity, coach them yourself or assign them to specific certified participants. If there is a large number of uncertified participants, repeat the activity by using volunteer coaches from the first round as the team leaders for the second round.

Team Teaching

For a quick demonstration of lecture games, I first divide participants into two groups. I make a two-minute presentation to one group on how to pronounce my first name. I then make a similar presentation to the other group on how to pronounce my last name. Finally, I have the members of each group pair up with members from the other group and have everyone coach his or her partner on how to pronounce my full name. That's Team Teaching.

Key Feature

Divide participants into two or more groups and then teach each group part of a procedure. Participants find partners from the other group(s), and teach their partners what they have learned. In this way, every participant acts as both a learner and a teacher.

When to Use This Format

Team Teaching has been particularly beneficial under the following circumstances:

- The instructional content involves a step-by-step procedure.
- Participants are capable of teaching and learning from each other.
- You have several application exercises.

Sample Topics

It's recommended you employ the Team Teaching method if your lecture topic is similar to one of these:

- how to construct a Pareto chart
- how to create an advertising slogan
- how to draw a flowchart
- how to solve a quadratic equation
- how to specify a performance objective
- how to write an executive summary.

Handouts

Provide the following handouts for your participants:

- description of the procedure
- application exercises.

Flow

Analyze the Procedure. Prior to the presentation, divide the procedure into steps. If there are more than six steps, organize them into three to six clusters of approximately equal complexity.

> *Laurie's presentation is on preparing a marketing plan. She decides that the procedure contains five major steps:*
>
> *1. specifying the market*
> *2. positioning the product*
> *3. determining the appropriate price*
> *4. selecting distribution channels*
> *5. promoting the product.*
>
> *Each step includes various activities. For example, promoting the product involves public relations, advertising, and participation in trade shows.*

Introduce the Procedure. Provide an overview of the procedure. Briefly describe each step and the interrelationship among the different steps.

> *Laurie uses a flow diagram to introduce the procedure for preparing a marketing plan. She spends 15 minutes giving a broad overview of the marketing plan.*

Form Groups. Have one group for each step or each cluster of steps, depending on the complexity of the presentation subject.

> *Because Laurie has five major steps in the procedure, she divides her participants into five groups. She schedules*

different 30-minute meeting times for the groups.

Present to the Groups. Each presentation deals with a single step or a cluster of steps assigned to that specific group. In addition, the presentation also identifies major links between one step and the others.

Laurie's presentation to the first group is about identifying different segments of the market. Using a word-processing program as an example, she walks the group through different activities for identifying the primary and secondary market segments. After a five-minute break at the end of the presentation, Laurie makes a presentation on the second step of positioning the product to the second group. Using the same procedure, she makes presentations to the remaining three groups on the remaining three steps.

Build Teams From Members of Different Groups. Each team should have one member from each of the different groups. This way, each team includes a person who has listened to each of the five presentations and thus has a member who is knowledgeable about each portion of the process.

Laurie creates the teams with one person from each group. Each team has a member who has listened to the presentation on specifying the market, positioning the product, determining the appropriate price, selecting distribution channels, and promoting the product.

Have Teams Perform a Task. Give the teams an application exercise. In completing the exercise, team members should teach each other the different steps of the procedure.

Laurie gives the teams several file folders with background information on a new soft drink and its market segments. She asks the teams to prepare a marketing plan.

Provide Consultative Help. While the teams are busy working on their project, walk around and provide help as needed.

Laurie spends three minutes with each team, observing their activities. Then she returns to different teams and provides just-in-time consultation.

Have Teams Give Reports. After teams have completed their project, ask each to give a brief report on their activities and accomplishments.

After an hour, Laurie invites the teams to give a five-minute report on what they have done and the problems that they faced. Laurie gives appropriate feedback, correcting some misconceptions and clarifying some of the steps.

Repeat the Procedure. Give teams additional application exercises. Make sure these exercises cover a wide variety of situations. Remind participants that they should learn all of the steps from each other while completing the exercises.

Laurie gives the teams another in-basket exercise, involving the marketing of a new toothpaste. While the teams are working on the project, she informally quizzes different members to ensure that they are learning all the steps.

What If...

There Is Not Enough Time? Spread this activity over several sessions. Give the initial presentation on the first day and the different presentations for different groups on following days. Have teams work on the application exercises the day after concluding presentations.

You Have to Handle All the Participants at Once? Use several people to make the different presentations. Have them deliver their lectures simultaneously. Be sure that you and your co-presenters use the same terminology.

You Don't Have Co-Presenters? Prepare a few participants ahead of time, teaching each of them one step or a cluster of steps. Have these participants teach the different groups later. As an alternative, videotape your presentation and show each team a different segment of the videotape.

Participants Cannot Be Divided Evenly Into Teams? Some teams may have more than one person who has listened to the same presentation. If some steps in the procedure are more difficult than others, put more than one participant into the team to handle that step. However, each team must have at least one representative from each mini-lecture.

Participants Don't Trust Their Peers? Explain to them that research on adult learners strongly demonstrates the power of team learning. Stress the fact that in the process of cooperative teaching and learning, everyone better understands the procedure.

Participants Focus Only on Their Own Step? Warn participants that they will have a final individual application exercise so they should focus for now on the group process.

Concluding Thoughts

If you assume that all training sessions should begin and end at specific times, you will have difficulty using these two powerful methods. If, however, you are willing to permit participants to complete their learning activities at their own pace, these methods will work effectively. In one of my client organizations, for example, several new-employee orientation skills (such as safety procedures) are taught continuously through the MLC format. Experienced (and certified) employees are encouraged to recruit and coach new employees in appropriate skills. One of the side effects of this approach is increased networking among all employees.

Major learning points in the interactive formats that we have explored so far come from the lecture presentation. The next chapter explores a different approach in which the learning points are embedded in an initial activity (such as a simulation) and the presentation is transformed into a debriefing discussion of participants' experience in the activity.

Debriefing

In reality, people do not learn from experience; they learn from reflecting on their experience. Debriefing is a systematic approach for encouraging participants to reflect on their experience and share their insights. The absence of debriefing is the main reason why exciting experiential activities, simulation games, role plays, and outdoor adventures fail to reach their maximum training effectiveness.

Begin with a jolt—a brief but powerful experiential exercise that catches participants behaving in a dysfunctional fashion. Follow up with a debriefing discussion to elicit and share useful insights and present relevant facts, concepts, and principles. This chapter delineates a great game to do just that:

- *Debriefing:* This method shows you how to follow experiential activities with effective discussion.

Debriefing

Simulation games, role playing, outdoor adventures, dramatic demonstrations, and other experiential activities provide highly motivating training. Unfortunately, however, their effectiveness is often dubious. The participants become excited, but they do not get the point. The Debriefing format follows experiential activities with an effective discussion to maximize their instructional value.

Key Feature

A debriefing discussion to elicit and share useful insights follows a brief and powerful experiential activity.

When to Use This Game

Debriefing is most effective in the following situations:

- The instructional content involves counterintuitive principles, attitudes, and values.
- Participants are capable of expressing their insights and feelings.
- You can use an appropriate experiential activity to dramatically demonstrate some important principle.

Sample Topics

Topics for which Debriefing would work well include those in the same genre as:

- cultural diversity
- everyday racism
- gender discrimination
- lateral thinking
- one-way communication
- shifting paradigms.

Handouts

Handouts and other items will vary from topic to topic when you are using the game

Debriefing. Be sure to incorporate and provide appropriate materials for the experiential activity during your interactive lecture.

Flow

Prepare for the Activity. Collect the necessary materials and supplies, and rehearse the activity. Be sure to identify the major learning points demonstrated by the activity.

Renato's presentation is on system archetypes as described in Peter Senge's article "The Learning Organisation: What Organisations Need to Do to Achieve Vision," which appeared in Thinkers magazine (Chartered Management Institute, March 1, 2002). Renato selects an experiential activity originally created by Martin Shubik, called Dollar Auction. Renato wants to highlight this learning point: Thoughtless responses to painful situations may escalate into a vicious cycle.

Conduct the Activity. Conduct your experiential activity without any lengthy introduction. Maintain a brisk pace throughout.

Renato holds up a dollar bill and explains that he is going to auction it off. The highest bidder will get the dollar. In addition, the second-highest bidder will also pay the amount he or she bid—but will not get anything in return.

The bidding begins at 50 cents and proceeds to 80 cents before the participants catch on to the fact that the second-highest bidder will lose money. Susie and Kevin keep the bids increasing to avoid ending up second. The auction becomes a heated bidding war between these two participants while the others remain silent and *enjoy the escalation. Eventually, the bidding stops at Susie's bid of $3.70. Renato collects the money from her and gives her the dollar bill. He also collects $3.60 from Kevin, the second-highest bidder.*

Introduce the Debriefing Session. Explain that different people may have gained different insights from participating in the experiential activity. Although everyone may be eager to express feelings and opinions, suggest a structured debriefing activity to maximize learning.

Renato announces that he is going to debrief the activity by leading a structured discussion. There will be seven stages; everyone will have plenty of opportunity to make their comments.

Gauge Reactions. Ask participants how they feel, providing an emotional outlet. Give them a chance to get intense feelings off their chests before objectively analyzing the experience.

Renato asks the participants to write down a word that describes their current feelings. He then asks them to predict what words other people may have written down. The suggested words include confused, manipulated, greedy, anxious, and puzzled. After observing that nobody seems to have a major need to further vent his or her feelings, Renato proceeds to the next debriefing stage.

Analyze What Happened. This question helps participants recollect the experiential activity. Ask follow-up questions to uncover the motivations behind people's behaviors.

Renato asks the participants to guess why some people participated in the bidding while others did not. Motives

included curiosity, impulsiveness, and greed. Renato then asks the participants for their guesses about why Susie bid the exorbitant amount of $3.70 for a dollar bill. Suggestions include the need to win, desire to avoid losing face, and unwillingness to give up.

Generalize From the Activity. Encourage participants to generalize from the activity. State some general principles, and ask participants whether they agree or disagree. Ask participants to provide evidence from either the experiential activity or real life to support or reject the principles.

Renato suggests that Dollar Auction ends up in a bidding war between two participants. Everybody agrees. He then suggests that men tend to bid more aggressively than women. Most participants disagree, citing Susie's behavior. One of the participants suggests that the Dollar Auction creates a vicious cycle. Most participants agree. Renato is successful because the group has focused on the learning point.

Make Real-World Connections. Help participants relate the activity to the real world. Ask them whether the activity reminds them of similar experiences. Follow this up by relating the general principles from the previous stage to situations that the participants are likely to encounter in their personal or professional lives.

Some participants relate the Dollar Auction to actual auctions. Others talk about wasting money to buy unnecessary items during a sale. Tom draws an analogy between bidding in the auction and drug addiction. Deb relates an incident involving an escalating personality conflict between two team members. Vicky points out that price wars are also examples of escalation.

Generally, lectures are given in auditoriums. The word "auditorium" comes from the Latin roots: "audio" meaning I hear and "taurus" meaning the bull.

Ask "What If" Questions. Use these questions to encourage participants to go beyond the data from the experiential activity.

Renato asks, "What if I auctioned $500?" and "What if the bidding was among teams rather than individuals?" Most participants believe that higher amounts would discourage escalation. They also believe that a group mentality and peer pressure would encourage teams to escalate their bids faster than individuals.

Ask How Participants Would Behave Differently. Ask whether they might change their behavior based on what they observed. Begin with changes in the behavior during the experiential activity. Later, ask about changes in real-world behavior.

Renato asks the participants how they might behave differently if he were to auction off another dollar bill. Most say they would just keep their mouths shut. A few others, however, want to get the mischief started and drop out when the bidding progresses to around 70 cents. One participant suggests that the bidders should talk to each other and agree to split their total loss equally. Renato praises this strategy and asks how it could apply in the real world.

Summarize. Take some time to collect insights, strategies, and real-world applications. Conclude the session with a summary of these key items. Be sure to include important principles and insights from previous sessions. This is a great way to improve the recall of the participants through repetition.

Renato summarizes the major discussion points and thanks everyone for their participation.

What If...

There Is Not Enough Time? Reduce the number of debriefing stages. For example, leave out some of the what-happened and what-if questions.

You Do Not Have a Suitable Experiential Activity? Get ideas from many of the free games and jolts available on my Website (www.thiagi.com) or check out books with collections of games. Look for dramatic demonstrations that you can conduct in a few minutes. Ask your colleagues for suggestions. At the next conference you attend, make a note of any dramatic demonstrations. Try designing your own mini-simulations.

You Are Worried About Conducting Experiential Activities? Remember that it is easier to conduct an experiential activity than to make a presentation because participants focus on the activity—not on you.

Concluding Thoughts

There are a couple of unique things about the debriefing format compared with the other interactive lecture formats: The presentation follows an experiential activity, and the major learning points are incorporated in the activity.

The key to the efficient use of debriefing lectures is to make sure that the initial activity does not take up so much time that you are forced to rush through the debriefing discussion. To ensure a rapid activity and leisurely debriefing, I recommend jolts—experiential activities that can be conducted in a few minutes but lend themselves to lengthy debriefing. You will find several jolts in the "Freebies" section of my Website (www.thiagi.com). You can incorporate these jolts into interactive lectures that use the debriefing format.

We have explored seven categories of interactive lectures, beginning with interspersed tasks and ending with debriefing. Does this mean that you have reached the end of the book—and the end of mastering interactive lecture formats?

No! Read on.

Not the End, but a Beginning

Welcome to the final chapter. I don't know how you got here. Perhaps you started from page one and dutifully progressed through the book, one page at a time. I hope not. Perhaps you read selectively, figured out how to use a couple interactive lecture formats and skipped to this chapter. If you are like me, perhaps you decided to jump straight to the last chapter first.

Whichever path you took, welcome.

A Thought Experiment

You probably have some questions and concerns about using the interactive lecture approach to your training situation. Even if you don't, pretend to be a cynic or a paranoid and do a bit of role playing for me. Write down a list of concerns you (or your cynical and risk-averse colleagues) have about interactive lectures. Write your list in the blank spaces below. If you run out of lines (or if you are planning to give this book to your boss as a gift), use a separate piece of paper.

Logic and Facts

Please do me a favor and email your list to thiagi@thiagi.com. Of course, I don't know exactly what you wrote in your list, but over the period of several years, I have collected different concerns from thousands of people who have attended my interactive lecture workshops. Here are their top dozen concerns and my responses:

1. *I don't have enough time to cover the training topics. Wasting time with participative activities will make it more difficult for me cover everything.* As a trainer, should you cover the content or should you help participants discover the content by encouraging them to explore the topic? If training is just telling, you can cover a great deal more by talking faster. But, surely there is more to training than merely presenting information within a given period of time. If you believe that training involves learning, retention, recall, and application, you need to encourage participants to take active responsibility. That is what interactive lectures enable you to do.

2. *I don't have time for all the additional preparation required for interactive lectures.* Bingo and Crossword are two interactive lecture formats that do require some additional preparation time. Perhaps you can save the time that you spend on preparing Power-Point slides and use it for creating Bingo cards or a Crossword puzzle. You may also use software programs to speed up the process. Most interactive lecture formats, though, do not need additional preparation time beyond the time you need for outlining your lecture. For example, Best Summaries requires you to merely make your usual presentation and follow it up by asking participants to write a summary of the key points.

3. *I have too many participants to effectively use these interactive lecture techniques.* Most interactive lectures can be used with groups of any size because the interaction involves individuals or two participants. In FAQs and Fakes, for example, you ask individual participants to come up with plausible answers to different questions and then let each person decide which answer is the "official" one. This activity can be conducted with large audiences without any need to organize them into teams. Even interactive lectures that require teamwork can be conducted in large groups by asking only a few teams to report out their conclusions.

4. *I have too few participants to use these interactive lecture techniques effectively.* Many interactive lecture formats can be used with only one to three participants. For example, you may use Press Conference with an individual participant by asking him or her to write a couple of questions on different topics, mixing them up with questions generated by earlier participants, and instructing your participant to select and sequence the questions for you to answer.

5. *Participants will talk about irrelevant things instead of discussing the training topic.* Most trainers (including me) are control freaks. They believe that only they know what topics are important and how to explain these topics. The reality, as shown in a large number of field studies on peer tutoring and coaching, is almost the exact opposite. When participants discuss training topics, they are better able to relate them to their own situation. Fellow participants are also much more capable of explaining different concepts and principles in their own language.

6. *Participants don't have enough knowledge to discuss the training topic in a meaningful fashion. They end up sharing their*

ignorance. In all interactive lectures, you combine lecture presentations with interactive discussions. You present some new content first and then ask participants to process it in different ways. In Interactive Interludes, for example, participants listen to a segment of your lecture and then paraphrase, disagree, apply, illustrate, personalize, or question the content. Don't be discouraged if you overhear participants revealing their misconceptions and errors. Treat this as valuable diagnostic information that permits you to provide appropriate corrections during the next segment of presentation.

7. *Participants don't have enough skills to complete the interactive tasks. I have to waste time training them on additional skills.* Some interactive lecture formats such as Idea Mapping require you to train participants on new skills (such as graphical note-taking). Once learned, participants can use these skills in future learning situations even beyond interactive lectures. Most interactive lectures, however, do not require new skills. In Words and Pictures, for example, all you ask the participants to do is to summarize the lecture in words or in pictures.

8. *Interactive lectures are so different that participants will become confused and uncomfortable.* It is true that Debriefing is a format that is very different from participants' expectations of a dull lecture or death-by-PowerPoint presentation. Usually, though, participants are pleasantly surprised. Even those who have some initial discomfort with an interactive lecture usually get used to the new format.

9. *Interactive lectures will not work in other countries and cultures where participants are accustomed to listening passively to lectures and taking notes.* I have conducted interactive lecture sessions in 25 different countries over extended periods of time. My friends and associates in different parts of the world regularly use interactive lectures. None of us have faced any major resistance. Once a trainer in any part of the world has successfully used an interactive lecture, he or she tends to expand the use of the method to more groups, more content areas, and more different formats. By the way, it is not only in other countries and cultures that participants expect passive training. This traditional mode is prevalent in all parts of the world, from Peoria to Pretoria and from New York to New Delhi.

10. *I am a technical trainer and interactive lectures will not work with my topics.* I originally used the interactive lecture approach for teaching physics. Most of my original design and field tests were conducted with trainers in high-tech areas involving such exotic topics such as microchip architecture. I used a series of interactive lectures in a workshop on financial analysis. During the past 20 years, my friends and associates have applied interactive lectures to a variety of topics in technical, managerial, sales, interpersonal, and product-knowledge areas.

11. *I don't know how to conduct the interactive activities. I feel afraid of losing control and making a fool of myself.* This book is designed to help you master the skills associated with interactive lectures. Don't try to learn several different formats in a single sitting. Just learn one format and apply it in your classroom.

12. *I cannot remember all of the steps in conducting an interactive lecture.* All you need to remember is the first step. While participants are busy interacting, you can remind yourself of the next step by referring to the Flow section for

Giving a lecture does not require any special competency or preparation. Any idiot can do it—and most idiots do.

each interactive lecture format described in this book. To make it easier, you may prepare an outline of the flow of activities on an index card and use it as a convenient job aid.

Does this list contain your concerns? The responses are not intended to laugh at your fears or browbeat you into changing your perceptions. They are just based on my experience and the experience of thousands of trainers who use the interactive lecture formats described in this book.

Three Key Points

Here are three generic, reassuring responses when you are worried about the use of interactive lectures:

1. You have a wide variety of interactive lecture formats at different levels of difficulty. Choose the format that best suits your topic, your audience, and your level of comfort.
2. Interactive lecture formats are flexible. You can speed them up or slow them

down. You can adjust them to accommodate different numbers of participants. This book explains how to make these adjustments with each different format.
3. Always remind yourself that your task is not to merely cover the content, but to help participants actively discover, understand, retain, recall, apply, and get excited about new principles and procedures.

Beyond Logic

My responses in the above section are factual and logical. However, it is probably not the lack of logical understanding that is causing your anxiety.

The best way to learn how to use interactive lectures is to use interactive lectures. So, choose a topic, choose a group, and choose an interactive lecture format. Conduct your first interactive lecture session tomorrow.

I guarantee that you are in for a pleasant surprise.

Handouts

This appendix contains reproducible masters for 11 handouts that are used in different interactive lecture formats.

As an individual purchaser of the book, you are granted free permission for paper reproduction of these handouts for training events. However, this permission does not allow you to make large-scale reproduction and distribution of more than 100 copies of each handout per year. Nor does this allow you to reproduce the handouts for sale or for other commercial use.

Please include the following copyright notice at the foot of each page that you reproduce:

Four of the handouts (3-3, 3-4, 6-1, and 6-2) deal with specific content areas (language simplification, defensive behaviors, reengineering, and leadership), and it is unlikely that you would want to use them in their current form. These handouts are included as examples to show how you can create similar handouts related to your own training topics.

All the other handouts deal with processes (such as writing questions or taking notes with Idea Maps) used by participants during interactive lectures. You may reproduce these handouts in their current form or modify them to suit the needs and preferences of your participants.

Handout 2-1. Template for closed questions.

Closed questions have a single correct answer; most require you to recall some fact. Even though multiple-choice and true/false formats are examples of closed questions, avoid them in this activity because they require recognition rather than recall of the correct answer.

The best way to ask a closed question is to start with one of the words or phrases shown in the following examples. To use any of these question forms, simply replace the words with strikethrough lines with words related to your content.

1. According to ~~Maslow~~, what is ~~the most basic human need~~?

2. How many ~~pages can be stored on a floppy disk~~?

3. How many ~~people are involved in the Quality Improvement Team~~?

4. How much ~~time is required to warm up the copying machine~~?

5. What is the first step ~~in evacuating the office building in case of fire~~?

6. What is the technical term for ~~reducing static electricity by using rubber gloves~~?

7. When is ~~the best time to give feedback to a co-worker~~?

8. Where is ~~the fire extinguisher located~~?

9. Who is ~~considered the Father of Performance Technology~~?

10. Why is it ~~dangerous to touch a light bulb with wet hands~~?

Handout 2-2. Template for open questions.

Open questions have more than one acceptable answer. However, you can compare two different answers to the same open question and decide which one is better.

Here are some examples of open questions. To use any of these question forms, simply replace the words with strikethrough lines with words related to your content.

1. Compare ~~laptops and pocket computers~~ in terms of ~~storage capacity~~.

2. How are ~~management~~ and ~~leadership~~ similar?

3. Give an example of ~~positive reinforcement~~.

4. How would you use ~~an incentive system~~?

5. How do you think ~~an Asian customer~~ will react to the ~~new model~~? Why do you think so?

6. How does ~~permission marketing increase our sales~~?

7. How does the ~~new incentive system~~ affect ~~marginal performers~~?

8. How does ~~the principle of reciprocity~~ apply to ~~customer complaints~~?

9. What are the implications of ~~declaring Fridays casual days~~?

10. What are the strengths of ~~teamwork~~?

11. What are the weaknesses of ~~teamwork~~?

12. What is an analogy for ~~immediate reinforcement~~?

13. What is an effective solution to the problem of ~~overcrowding in subways~~?

14. What is the best ~~strategy for telemarketing~~? Why?

15. What is the difference between ~~management~~ and ~~leadership~~?

16. What is the meaning of ~~"digital capital"~~?

17. What is the primary cause of ~~violence in the workplace~~? Why?

18. What would happen if ~~you ignore customer complaints~~?

19. Why does ~~punishment~~ produce ~~unpredictable effects~~?

20. Why is ~~customer loyalty~~ important?

Handout 2-3. Poster contest instructions I.

Your job is to design a poster that presents the key points of this section of the lecture. Here are the four rules:

1. *Page limit:* You are limited to one sheet of flipchart paper.

2. *Words only:* Your poster must use only words. You may not use any graphics, pictures, or diagrams.

3. *Joint effort:* All team members should contribute to the creation of the poster.

4. *Time limit:* The final version of the poster should be ready in five minutes.

Handout 2-4. Poster contest instructions II.

Your job is to design a poster that presents the key points of this section of the lecture. Here are the four rules:

1. *Page limit:* You are limited to one sheet of flipchart paper.

2. *Pictures only:* Your poster must use only pictures including graphics, symbols, icons, or diagrams without words. You may not use any letters, words, or numbers.

3. *Joint effort:* All team members should contribute to the creation of the poster.

4. *Time limit:* The final version of the poster should be ready in five minutes.

Handout 3-1. How to use Idea Mapping.

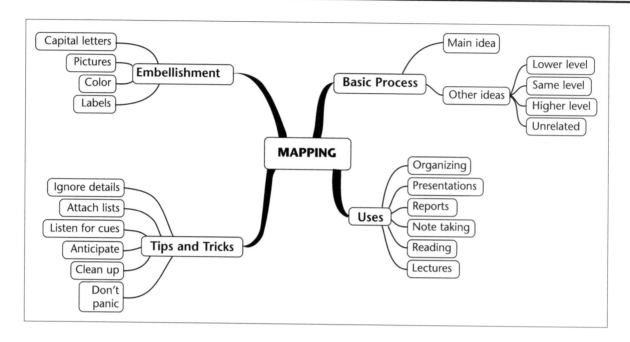

Basic Procedures

1. *Main idea:* Place the main idea or the session's in capital letters inside a circle in the middle of the page.

2. *Subsequent ideas:* Think of other ideas related to the main idea. Write them inside circles, and link each circle to the main idea.

3. *Lower level:* During the later stages of mapping, if you identify another idea at a lower level, place it inside a circle. Connect this idea to the current idea.

4. *Same level:* If you identify another idea at the same level, place it inside a circle. Connect this idea to the same idea to which the current idea is linked.

5. *Higher level:* If you identify another idea at a higher level, place it inside a circle on an equal level with Basic Process and Uses and link it to mapping.

6. *Unrelated ideas:* If an idea appears to be unrelated to any of the previous ideas, leave it out of the circle or start a new page with this idea placed in the center as a main idea.

Embellishing the Map

1. *Capitals and underlining:* Indicate the importance of an idea by the use of capital letters and underlining.

2. *Pictures, symbols, and shapes:* Whenever appropriate, use visuals instead of words. Use simple pictures and cartoon figures to represent an idea. Use various symbols such as exclamation points and stars. Instead of using circles for all the ideas, use different shapes to indicate different levels of ideas.

3. *Color:* Various colors can be used to identify different branches in your map.

4. *Labels for lines:* Whenever appropriate, label the line to indicate the relationship. For example, you may label a line connecting "solar system" and "Jupiter" as "is a part of."

Handout 3-1. How to use Idea Mapping (continued).

Uses of Mapping

1. *Organizing and outlining:* Use the mapping technique to organize your information into an outline.

2. *Presentations:* Idea Maps can provide useful outlines for your presentations.

3. *Reports:* Use Idea Maps to outline an article or a report you are preparing.

4. *Note taking:* Use the Idea-Mapping technique—instead of the traditional linear outlining approach—for taking notes.

5. *Reading:* Use Idea Maps for taking notes on what you are reading. You can use the headings and side headings of your readings to suggest appropriate ideas and links.

6. *Lectures:* Use Idea Maps to take notes while you are listening to a lecture. When you use Idea Mapping for note-taking during lectures, you have to work fast.

Tips and Tricks

1. *Don't panic:* Even if you're not keeping pace with the lecture, you don't have to panic about missing important ideas. Remember you listen and think much faster than the presenter speaks.

2. *Ignore details:* Do not try to map everything the presenter is saying. Look for key concepts and ideas rather than minute details.

3. *Attach lists:* In addition to the main ideas in circles, you can prepare lists of steps or details. Place these in a corner of the Idea Map or record them on an attached page.

4. *Listen for cues:* During the lecture, listen for cues about main ideas and related ideas. For example, if the lecturer prefaces a statement by saying "First" you can be sure that what will follow is either a main idea or the first step in a procedure.

5. *Anticipate and review:* If there are long periods without new ideas during the presentation—for example, if the presenter is telling a lengthy anecdote—use some of your time to review what you have already mapped. Add additional links and clean up the map. Also use the time to anticipate what the lecturer is likely to say next.

6. *Clean up the map:* As soon as possible after the lecture, review the ideas and links in your map. If necessary, redraw the map on a new page to make it easier to read.

Learning to Map

1. *Begin with an outline:* Start with a map that will organize information you already know. For example, create a self-portrait map. Place a circle with the word "me" in the middle of a page and begin mapping important information about yourself.

2. *Practice Idea Mapping an article:* For your next exercise, read an article and map its contents. It is more challenging to recapture the organization of an article than to organize your own thoughts.

3. *Map the content of an audiotape recording:* To get practice with Idea Mapping a lecture, record it before mapping. That way you can pause, rewind, and map the same section repeatedly. This will provide excellent practice in Idea Mapping. Eventually, you should be able to Idea Map in real time while listening to a lecture.

Handout 3-2. Intelligent Interruptions.

You have 30 seconds to prepare for one of the following types of interruptions. Remember that your interruption should relate to the most recent segment of the presentation. Your interruption should last for at least 30 seconds and not more than one minute.

1. *Apply:* Present a personal action plan and explain how you would implement the strategies and techniques.

2. *Disagree:* Identify flaws in and raise major issues with the ideas presented. Offer your dissenting opinions.

3. *Illustrate:* Come up with real or imaginary examples of the concepts and principles.

4. *Paraphrase:* Summarize the key points.

5. *Personalize:* Share your personal reactions.

6. *Question:* Ask five or more questions about—and beyond—the content. Explain why you consider these important questions for the presenter to answer.

Handout 3-3. Aida's handout.

Language Simplification Checklist

☐	Word length	Use simple and short words.
☐	Proper nouns	Use short, well-known names.
☐	Pronouns	Make sure all pronouns have clear antecedents.
☐	Technical terms	Use them only when necessary.
☐	Definitions	Define technical terms the first time you use them.
☐	Examples	Use them to define technical terms.
☐	Special meanings	When using a common word in a special sense, define this special meaning first.
☐	Nouns and verbs	Keep them distinct from each other.
☐	Idioms	Avoid idiomatic expressions and verb phrases.
☐	Sentence length	Keep your sentences short and simple.
☐	Sentence structure	Avoid complex and compound sentences.
☐	Verb tense	Use the simple tenses.
☐	Voice	Use the active voice.
☐	Sentence order	Use the normal word order.
☐	Clarity	Remove all unnecessary qualifying phrases.
☐	Visuals	Use diagrams to clarify complex information.

Handout 3-4. An example of a glossary that could be used during Role Play.

Defensive Behaviors	Nondefensive Behaviors
Denial: Refusing to accept responsibility by denying your fault.	*Acceptance:* Taking the responsibility for your mistake and offering to make amends.
Partial acceptance: Accepting responsibility for one part of the problem (usually a trivial part), and denying the rest of the problem.	*Apology:* Expressing regrets for your mistake and for the inconvenience it caused.
Excuses: Blaming the problem on various factors outside your control.	*Problem definition:* Working with the other person to clarify the problem caused by your mistake.
Counterattack: Diverting the attention from your faults by pointing out that the other person has committed the same mistakes or similar mistakes.	*Planning:* Working with the other person to specify what needs to be done to minimize the damage caused by your mistake.
Mind reading: Implying that the other person has ulterior motives for pointing out your faults.	*Listening:* Paying undivided attention to the other person. Trying to understand what the other person is saying and feeling.
Whining: Acting like an innocent victim of circumstances and implying that the other person should not be picking on you.	*Valuing:* Expressing your feeling that a return to the positive relationship is very important to you.
Withdrawing: Expressing your need to get out of the relationship with the other person because you are pessimistic about the future.	*Validating:* Confirming the right of the other person to feel frustrated, disappointed, or angry at your behavior.
	Mirroring: Identifying the other person's feelings and emotions and indicating your awareness of these feelings.

Handout 5-1. Scoring sheet for Shouting Match.

Attitude Rating Value	Number of People	Attitude Rating Value x Number of People
1		
2		
3		
4		
5		
6		
7		
8		
9		
Totals:		

Average = Total from last column ÷ Total from middle column

Handout 6-1. Vartan's list of reengineering rules.

1. Don't follow any rules. Challenge them!

2. Don't accept assumptions. Question them!

3. Don't analyze the existing process. Start from scratch!

4. Don't be cheap. Bet your bottom dollar!

5. Don't centralize. Don't decentralize. Use distributive computing!

6. Don't check. Don't control. Don't reconcile. Let people be!

7. Don't create new jobs. Combine existing ones!

8. Don't fix it. Change it!

9. Don't follow rules. Question them!

10. Don't go for continuous improvement. Go for radical changes!

11. Don't hide information. Share your data!

12. Don't involve experts. Hire naive people!

13. Don't maintain functional departments. Create process teams!

14. Don't pay for performance. Pay for results!

15. Don't supervise. Coach!

16. Don't train. Educate!

17. Don't use experts. Use expert systems!

Handout 6-2. Leadership questions submitted to Jin.

1. How does a leader communicate effectively with all followers (or employees)? Is it ever possible for a leader to communicate directly with all of his or her followers?

2. How does an effective leader cope with complexity and ambiguity?

3. How does a leader empower his followers while demanding accountability?

4. Is there a difference between the skills required for the leader of a small team and the leader of a large organization?

5. Is there a difference between the leader of a nonprofit organization and a for-profit organization? If so, what is it?

6. Does gender play a role in leadership?

7. Many people claim that integrity is an important leadership quality. What exactly does this mean? Who are some current leaders with integrity?

8. Most leadership literature stresses the importance of unwaveringly pursuing a goal. Does this not make a leader rigid and inflexible?

9. Should the leader of a corporation also be a technical expert?

10. U.S. presidents in the recent past appear to have violated key leadership principles. How did they get elected and how did they survive?

11. The workplace is become more global and multicultural. What implications does this have for leaders of the future?

12. What are the differences between a national leader and a multinational leader?

13. What are the major differences between a leader and a manager? Is it possible for the same person to function effectively as both?

14. What are the major differences between current leadership principles and previous leadership principles?

15. What are the steps in leading a major change in an organization? How does the leader make sure that the change continues for a long time?

16. What is the best way for a leader to come up with a strategic plan? How does the leader sell this plan to his followers?

17. What is the difference between a leader and a coach?

18. What is the relationship between trust and leadership?

19. What role does charisma play in leadership? Is it possible for a leader without charisma to function effectively?

20. Which is more important: having a clear vision or being able to communicate one's vision?

Additional Resources

Antion, T. (1997). *Wake 'Em Up: How to Use Humor and Other Professional Techniques to Create Alarmingly Good Business Presentations.* Anchor: Landover Hills, MD, and Creative Training Techniques Press: Minneapolis, MN.

Booher, D. (2003). *Speak With Confidence: Powerful Presentations That Inform, Inspire, and Persuade.* McGraw-Hill: New York.

Bowman, S. (2003). *Preventing Death by Lecture! Terrific Tips for Turning Listeners Into Learners.* Beauperson Publishing Company: Glenbrook, NV.

Denning, S. (2001). *The Springboard: How Storytelling Ignites Action in Knowledge-Era Organizations.* Butterworth-Heinemann: Boston.

Gargiulo, T.L. (2002). *Making Stories: A Practical Guide for Organizational Leaders and Human Resource Specialists.* Quorum: Westport, CT.

Hoff, R. (1996). *Say It in Six: How to Say Exactly What You Mean in 6 Minutes or Less.* Barnes & Noble: New York.

Hoff, R. (1997). *Do Not Go Naked into Your Next Presentation: Nifty Little Nuggets to Quiet the Nerves and Please the Crowd.* Andrews & McMeel: Kansas City, MO.

Jeary, T., K. Dower, and J.E. Fishman. (2004). *Life Is a Series of Presentations: 8 Ways to Punch Up Your People Skills at Work, at Home, Anytime, Anywhere.* Simon & Schuster: New York.

Johnstone, K. (1999). *Impro for Storytellers.* Routledge: New York.

Koppett, K. (2001). *Training to Imagine: Practical Improvisational Theatre Techniques to Enhance Creativity, Teamwork, Leadership, and Learning.* Stylus: Sterling, VA.

Leech, T. (2004). *How to Prepare, State, and Deliver Winning Presentations.* American Management Association: New York.

Peoples, D.A. (1992). *Presentations Plus: David Peoples' Proven Techniques.* John Wiley & Sons: New York.

Rozakis, L. (1999). *The Complete Idiot's Guide to Public Speaking.* Alpha: New York.

Underhill, R. (2000). *Khrushchev's Shoe and Other Ways to Captivate Audiences from One to One Thousand.* Perseus: Cambridge, MA.

Wacker, M.B., and L.L. Silverman. (2003). *Stories Trainers Tell: 55 Ready-To-Use Stories To Make Training Stick.* Jossey-Bass/Pfeiffer: San Francisco.

Walters, L. (1993). *Secrets of Successful Speakers: How You Can Motivate, Captivate, and Persuade.* McGraw-Hill: New York.

Walters, L. (1995). *What to Say When . . . You're Dying on the Platform: A Complete Resource for Speakers, Trainers, and Executives.* McGraw-Hill: New York.

Weissman, J. (2003). *Presenting to Win: The Art of Telling Your Story.* Financial Times Prentice Hall: Upper Saddle River, NJ.

About the Author

Sivasailam "Thiagi" Thiagarajan has been a high-school physics teacher, street-corner magician, social activist, author, instructional designer, educational researcher, project director for the U.S. Agency for International Development, and a consultant. He is currently the resident mad scientist at the Thiagi Group, an organization that specializes in improving human performance effectively and enjoyably.

Thiagi is known for his faster, cheaper, and better approaches to performance-based instructional design. He has designed online and facilitator-led instructional packages in different media and methods for different types of participants. As a specialist in training games and simulations, Thiagi has created hundreds of training games, including the classic cross-cultural simulation, "Barnga." He has also published several books of games and how-to manuals on game design.

Thiagi is a regular presenter at professional conferences and is active in professional organizations. He has been the president of the International Society for Performance Improvement (ISPI) twice and president of the North American Simulation and Gaming Association (NASAGA) four times.

Thiagi has lived in three different countries and cultures (India, the United States, and Liberia) for several years and has consulted, trained, and facilitated in 25 other countries.